The Marriage Cure

A Couple Therapy Workbook to Fighting Anxiety in Love, Strengthening Your Relationship and Building a Lasting Couple Life

By Gary Wayne

Introduction

"A successful marriage requires falling in love many times, always with the same person." Those were the words of Mignon Mclaughlin, a famous journalist, and author. Marriage is considered the next step in a serious relationship, a ceremony conducted with the friends and family of the couple to celebrate their union and the decision to spend the rest of their lives together. Many women dream about their perfect wedding dress and perfect wedding ceremony since they were little, as well as men will search for the perfect ring to purpose as soon as they meet the right woman they want to have with them always.

In the past, marriage used to be an arrangement between families. For example, in ancient times, marriage was used as a tool for power. Kings and princes married to seal an alliance or enhance the power of their kingdoms. In other words, it was a beneficial union. The view of marriage as a beneficial union still existed in the not so distant past, where families married off their daughters and sons to someone who was rich, had power, and earned the family the much needed, for some reason prestige.

Today, couples have the freedom to meet with someone, develop a relationship, and marry whenever they feel they are ready. They don't have to marry out of force but out of choice. This freedom, however, has become a double-edged sword. The divorce rates have risen dramatically and more marriages are ending due to several factors and not all of them are attributed to serious reasons.

However, it is even difficult to create specific rules that apply to all people and guide them through to develop a marriage that will not end in a divorce. This is happening because we are talking about people and every person is different. The only thing we can do is offer to every person that decides to marry advice, derived from the reports and mistakes that have been previously done by others.

For example, we see today people marry after a few months of dating. Those marriages have higher chances of ending in divorce than those of people who have been together for years. Still, this does not mean that people who have been in a serious relationship for many years will not get divorced just that they have a lower chance of doing so. One obvious reason for this is that the couple who has been together for years would be able to go through many difficult times together and were able to develop a communication system to resolve the issues that may arise.

This book aims to provide the necessary information needed to build a relationship that will lead to a strong marriage. In the first chapter, we will present the different types of relationships to help you pinpoint in which category you and your partner mostly belongs in. In the second chapter, we will analyze the different types of men that exist so as to guide you through which types of men suit your needs better and which are not build for serious relationships before making the decision to get married to your partner. However, keep in mind that you are the one who knows your partner better and if you have already made up your mind, the good for you!

In the third chapter, we will present you with the different types of women because women may dream of their wedding since they were little girls, but there are also those that can be a little difficult to deal with at first and may pose a challenge to many of their partners. In the fourth chapter, we will present you with the different characteristics that will help you build a solid foundation for your relationship that will later lead to a solid marriage.

In the fifth chapter, we will present you with all the common problems that married couples face that have higher chances of ending the relationship in divorce. In the sixth chapter, we will present you with the various things you should do before getting married that will help you through the process and your shared lives. I do hope you will like this journey inside the relationship world.

Chapter 1: The Different Types of Relationships

When we talk about the relationship a person has with other people, we refer to the interaction, association, bond, and connection between two or more individuals. Generally, there are four types of relationships:

- ✓ Family Relationships
- ✓ Friendships
- ✓ Acquaintanceships
- ✓ Romantic Relationships

Family relationships have to do with the people we are connected through some form of kinship. This could be done through blood, as it happens with our parents and other siblings, through marriage, as it happens with non-blood related step-parents step-siblings and uncles with aunts or through adoption. Family refers to parents and siblings you see every day as you grow up as well as other relatives such as grandparents, cousins, uncles, and aunts, you may not see as frequently as your parents and siblings.

There many forms of families such as stepfamilies, homes with lesbian or gay parents, and single-parent ones. It would be ideal if people maintained strong relationships with their families, even though this is not always the case. People should grow up learning how to love their relatives to feel as comfortable as possible to seek their help and confide in them personal feelings and thoughts. It is a known fact that parents along with older relatives are asked with offering support, guidance, and teach their child the meaning of boundaries and the importance of self-discipline.

It is very logical for families to have to deal with disagreements and arguments since they spend very much time together and are extremely close. However, those problems should not last long and even when a person is hurt or angry, families stick together since they care and love each other. The relationship of a family lasts for a lifetime, even if children turn into teenagers and then to adults. At these times the relationship changes and children will be more independent. Then, the relationship with the parents will become one that is characterized by mutual support and less one that is tasked to guide a child. Teenage years may present parents with many problems since this is the time when a child will try to find his adult identity and gain his or her independence from the parents. Those attempts may leade to more conflicts and arguments that are usually over when the teenage years are over.

It is very important for family members to be able to communicate and nurture a healthy relationship, thus forging a source of support that will last for a lifetime. In some families, physical contact is rare and choose to express their love in other ways, while other families choose to express their love with affection moves such as kissing on the forehead or cheek, tousling the hair, hugging, patting on the back, among other things.

Family relationships are extremely important because they can affect the ability someone has to form other kinds of relationships when they grow up. Family relationships will be the first model a child has through which he or she may build on the rest of the relationships this child will develop as an adult such as friendships and romantic ones. Sometimes people fail in romantic relationships because they are afraid of forming a relationship that is similar to the parental one or they are trying to find the seemingly perfect parental relationship, thus leave any relationships that show signs of little imperfection.

Moving on to friendships, friends are the people who choose to come into contact with and are not related to us. A friend is someone we care about, we feel comfortable enough to confide in, we respect, and trust. Having a good friendship means having a relationship that is based on reciprocity, loyalty, support, and honesty. Reciprocity means that for a friendship to exist, both people must see the other as a friend. There are various levels of friendship since you may feel closer to some of your friends than you feel with others, especially if you haven't known some for a very long time.

New friends may not feel comfortable to trust you yet with their personal problems or issues and in return, this may be the case for you too. This is most certainly normal since you have known each other for a short time and you may even not get together very often. You will be more comfortable to speak about your personal problems with friends whom you know for a longer time and spend more time in their company. The friends you are most comfortable with and know for the longest time are most often referred to as best friends. There are some people who have many friends and others who choose to have few. Both cases are normal since there is no rule or the right number of friends you should have. Keep in mind that every person is different.

Friends are respectful towards each other and offer support. Thy most usually have common ideas and interests. Some friends choose to show their love with kissing on the cheek or hugging while other friends show less physical contact. Friendships are also important when trying to develop a romantic relationship since many people hold the opinion of their friends in high regard. There have been many cases when a relationship was ruined due to friends and romantic partners who were not getting along at all.

Friends are the family we choose for ourselves, but it is important to remember that in a relationship there are only two people. While the opinion of our friends is important and sometimes they have saved us from bad choices, it would be wise to not always follow the opinion of other people regarding our personal affairs.

If someone makes the wrong choice in a romantic partner, this was a personal choice and he or she will move on with the support of friends.

Acquaintances are usually people we encounter often, but we do not see them as friends or family. People that we call acquaintances may be a neighbor, a group of people we work with or someone we met at a party and have seen a number of times at a social event but we are not too familiar with yet. It is important to be respectful and polite to our acquaintances as a way to avoid conflict and stress that will occur if we are disrespectful towards them.

Do not forget that from this group of people, we may later develop friendships or romantic relationships. Almost always we have developed those relationships from people we previously considered as acquaintances.

A romantic relationship is almost always characterized by a person who feels very fond of and attracted to another person both on a physical and mental level. In order to be called a romantic relationship, both people should feel the same way about the other. When they are not living together and are often apart, they will stay in contact through social media or their phones and will want to see each other frequently.

Both partners that have formed a romantic relationship will admit they are attracted and that they are in love with each other. It is possibly the closest type of relationship that forge a very strong bond and connection that they do not have with anyone else. For this reason, this connection will be monogamous and exclusive. For someone to have a successful romantic relationship it must be based on support, desire for the people involved, trust, acceptance, respect, and shared interests.

Some people who are involved in a romantic relationship may choose to spend their lived together and have children. In romantic relationships various types of physical contact are acceptable that would not be right in other types of relationships such as kissing on the lips, sexual relations, prolonged cuddling, and holding, as long as they are all mutually agreed on by both parties involved.

In romantic relationships, there will be arguments as well as disagreements. If those are within the logical boundaries and do not include abusive behaviors, in strong relationships, they will be resolved through compromise, effective communication, and understanding. However, if those arguments are frequent the partners involved will decide to terminate their relationship. In some relationships, it is apparent rather quickly that the people involved are not compatible with each other and the relationship is terminated before any serious feelings are developed. In other cases, people stay together forever.

Independent Relationships

Romantic relationships can be further categorized into different types. The first type we will briefly analyze is the Independent relationship. In an independent relationship, there are two people who lead two separate lives and have one common life. The two partners are completely independent people who do not rely on their partner for anything. They are what most people call "power couple".

However, in these types of relationships, the two partners are in danger of making several mistakes. For example, they may feel the need to not compromise for anything and do not know the meaning of sacrifice for the relationship. They may not accept the fact that they shouldn't leave their clothes on the couch since this is angering their partner or they do not accept the fact that they should cut down their work hours for a while because their partner feels neglected.

Also, in an independent relationship, one partner may instinctively place himself or herself above the needs and desires of the other partner and or both partners may indulge in this behavior. For example, they may never go to meet with their partner if he or she needs to see them if the independent person is tired or has something better to do at his or her standards. In extreme cases, love will not be a top priority, they will lead completely separate social lives, and will be essentially focused only on their careers.

But not all independent relationships seem as if the partners care only for themselves. A level of independence in relationships is needed so as to not become drowned in the other person and forget who we are. A healthy independent relationship will include the two partners setting healthy and clear boundaries since each person is his or her own source of strength, and the ability to be an individual.

They understand that each person is unique with their own needs and characteristics. Also, despite the admission that each person is unique, the independent partners come together for a common purpose which is passion and partnership. They see each other as an extension of themselves; they are still a separate person but come together to fulfill a purpose set by them.

You could think of a healthy independent relationship as two individual parts coming together to create a third one. For example, their strength, energy, and effectiveness are greater when they are together and this is the reason why they are often viewed as a power couple. The needs and desires of one partner cannot be set above the needs of the other partner. Their communication takes time to build and needs effort from both sides, but when it is set then, it is perfect. They are able to avoid misunderstandings from the start before they turn into serious problems.

Also, they know how to compromise when it is truly needed. Each independent partner knows when he or she should get out of their comfort zone and even feel some discomfort to succeed in a relationship as long as it is within logic. They want to evolve through the relationships and this is done by placing trust in each partner and know that the experiences they share with each other are fulfilling and with meaning.

Co-dependent Relationships

The next type of romantic relationship we will briefly analyze are co-dependent relationships. In this type, both partners just can't function without each other. They can't be apart for too long. Co-dependent relationships are the exact opposite of independent relationships. Not being able to be away from your partner can cause many problems. In a relationship, the partners should be independent; they should maintain their personality and keep in mind that they existed before the relationship existed.

This type of relationship is usually characterized by a person making a lot of sacrifices for the happiness of the other partner, but they do not get much in return. According to experts, it is a pattern behavior where a person is dependent on someone else and seeks their approval in order to validate their identity and self-worth. The most apparent sign is when you feel as if your purpose in life revolves around making great sacrifices to fulfill the needs of your partner.

In the words of Scott Wetzler who is chief of the psychology division at Albert Einstein College of Medicine, "Codependent relationships signify a degree of unhealthy clinginess, where one person doesn't have self-sufficiency or autonomy. One or both parties depend on their loved ones for fulfillment."

Any person can become codependent. Research suggests that people who were emotionally abused or neglected by their parents are at a higher chance of forming codependent relationships. According to Shawn Burn who is a psychology professor at California Polytechnic State University, San Luis Obispo, "These kids are often taught to subvert their own needs to please a difficult parent, and it sets them up for a long-standing pattern of trying to get love and care from a difficult person."

- ✓ The signs of you being in a co-dependent relationship include:
- ✓ The person is not getting satisfaction from his or her life outside of the relationship.

- ✓ The person recognizes that his or her partner shows unhealthy behaviors, but stay with him or her despite those.
- ✓ They support their partner at the expense of their own emotional, physical, and mental health.

According to psychologist Seth Meyers, "Individuals can also assume they are in a codependent relationship if people around them have given them feedback that they are too dependent on their partner or if they have a desire, at times, for more independence but feel an even stronger conflict when they attempt to separate in any way."

A co-dependent relationship will have a negative impact on the other relationships and needs of one partner. The one partner who is dependent or in case both partners are dependent on each other, they will be exhausted by constantly trying to meet the needs of the other person and he or she will neglect their other relationships. The dependent person is the enabler since he or she is the one who maintains the dysfunctions and irrationalities of the other person.

To be able to change all that, experts recommend that the couple should talk about their feelings and set goals for their relationship that are satisfactory for both of them. According to psychologist Misty Hook, " "It's also important to spend time with relatives, friends, and family to broaden the circle of support," she says.

"Find hobbies of your own. Try separating for certain periods of time to create a healthy dependence on one another."

Dominant or Submissive Relationship

The next type of relationship is the dominant or submissive relationship. This relationship is characterized by the controlling behavior of one partner that has no boundaries and another person who submits to the rules and demands of that partner, no matter how absurd these rules may seem. For example, a demand he or she may make is that you are not allowed to go out with your friends without him or even cut off all your male friends. This type of relationship will have the submissive partner be filled with anxiety since he or she will not be able to give voice to their thoughts or make their needs and demands clear to the dominating partner. This relationship type also lacks trust, independence, and trust, things that are essential to building a healthy and good relationship.

There are many signs of a dominating partner and most of us think of them as people who are making threats, give ultimatums, are physically aggressive, and are essentially a bully. Those are indeed signs of a person being dominating, but you will also be able to read many more cues on his or her behavior that show their domineering nature. Some partners that want to control everything are doing so out of an emotional vulnerability they feel and are afraid of rejection.

There are times when they have mastered the emotional manipulation to the extent that their partner who is controlled, thinks that they are the ones who do something wrong and are at fault. They are made to believe that they are extremely lucky their dominating partner puts up with them. No form of abuse is acceptable and this is emotional abuse, so the relationship is not a healthy one.

Some other signs of a controlling partner are the following:

Isolating the submissive partner from family and friends: This sign may start out very subtly, but it is considered by experts as the first sign of a dominating person. They may start with complaints about how often you are speaking with your siblings over the phone or confess that they don't like your friends and you shouldn't go out with them because they are dragging you to a dark path. Essentially, they will try to isolate you from anyone that used to support you and be close to you prior to your relationship. Their goal of doing this is to strip you of the ones that could be there for you and advise you to leave this dominating relationship, thus leaving you open to emotional abuse where you will not be able to stand up for yourself.

Continuous criticism, even for simple things: Just like isolations, criticism can also begin in a subtle way. The submissive partner will actually think that their partner is trying to make them a better person through this criticism or even try to find some kind of logic behind the comments such as that it is logical their partner does not like the way they decorate, dress, or speak. This behavior will make the submissive partner feel as if it is tough to be accepted or loved and every little thing they will do will be based on the premise that the submissive partner must do everything in his or her power to improve their position on their partner's eyes so as to see them as an equal and finally love them back.

Making threats against you or them: Threats do not only have to do with physical abuse. Threats can be made also by cutting off certain "privileges" or by a dominating partner threatening to harm themselves. Both cases are aiming for emotional manipulation. There are many cases of people being stuck in a relationship because they are afraid their partner will do something to harm themselves if they were about to leave. Other threats that can be made involve losing access to children or losing their home and even financial support if the submissive partner leaves.

Making love conditional: Essentially, the controlling partner will make you feel as if you are not good enough. He or she may say: "I am not in the mood of being intimate with you. However, if you lose weight and work out, I will," "I love you so much more when you are successful at work," "You can't even make dinner. I don't know why I am even in this relationship."

Making guild their weapon: Many dominating partners are excellent at manipulation and manage to make the emotions of the submissive person work in their favor. They will manipulate them into feeling guilty for everything they want to achieve. Be it staying inside, not going for vacations with friends, not visiting family, anything they want to get, they will use manipulation.

Make you feel indebted to them: Dominating partners at first will shower their partner with expensive gifts, show their intentions of creating a serious commitment, will take their partner out to luxurious places and adventurous things. We hope these are done because the guy is Mr. Perfect, but sometimes those gestures are used as leverage for control. When the time is right and you refuse them something they want, they will make you feel as if you owe them for everything they have done for you and given you.

Know more than they are entitled to: A dominating partner will make demands to know things they are not entitled to unless the other partner wants to show them. For example, they will keep snooping and demand that you share with them personal information. They will even check your phone, track your

23

internet history, check your emails, and similar things. When you ask them about it, they will tell you that they have been burned before and have trust issues. They could even tell you that since you have nothing to hide, you wouldn't mind them snooping around. This is a violation of privacy and no boundaries have been set. They are not interested in trying to trust you and you wouldn't want a police department in your relationship.

Paranoia and overactive jealousy: At the beginning of a relationship, jealousy can be taken as flattery is an endearing trait since it is considered as a sign that your partner cares for you and he or she feels committed. However, if your partner sees every move you make as flirting and is threatened by the people you interact with may be anxious, paranoid, and insecure. Do not reward this behavior and let it develop into your relationship, this is also an attempt of control.

Not respecting that you need some time alone: The dominating partner will make you feel guilty any time you express your need to have some alone time to recuperate. They will make you feel as if you don't love them enough since, to their mind, you will need less time with them and more time for yourself. In healthy relationships, there is effective communication in such matters and in the end, there will be a compromise. In controlling relationships, the person who needs to have some time for themselves will be presented as the one being at fault and denied their need to be alone.

They will make you earn trust and other good behaviors: It is only logical that you will trust a partner more when you have dated him or her for many years than the partner whom you have only dated for a month, but for a relationship to work, there should be a certain amount of trust in the relationship. For example, you shouldn't have to report every move you make and every place you have been during your day, and your partner shouldn't feel entitled to having access to your personal information and belongings such as your internet history, texts, and emails. If your partner makes you think that trust is something to be earned in such ways rather than being something it already exists at the start of the relationship, then the dynamic is not looking good. Trust needs to be earned when it is lost. When you start a relationship you trust your partner until he or she has done something that proves otherwise.

They think you are guilty until proven innocent: We have already established that a dominating partner has the necessary skills to make you feel guilty about something they think you have done wrong. You may encounter them after you return from work, already angry and with evidence of something you have done wrong during your absence. They will withhold those evidence until they make you feel as if you indeed have done something wrong. They will keep doing this because they want to have something based on which they will push you from making this mistake again, according to them, and keep your behavior towards them as it is.

They will make you tired of arguing until you give in: Many controlling people keep arguing with their partners openly and constantly at every chance they get when they think they are not getting their way. This is especially the case when the submissive partner is almost always passive and the domineering partner gets his or her way in every disagreement they have. Usually, this is the case when the submissive partner wants to avoid conflicts by nature and feels exhausted by all the arguments that have taken place between them.

Make you feel as if you are unworthy of them: They will start by making you feel less attractive than they are or keep bragging about their professional achievements when he or she compares them to yours. They may even start bragging about their exes since controlling partners will want to make you feel grateful and lucky you managed to get them into a relationship with you. In turn, with this behavior, they will force you to work harder in order to keep them happy and satisfied to prevent them from finding someone else and leave you. This dynamic is the dream of every controlling partner.

Teasing that has an uncomfortable undertone: Teasing and humor are believed to be an essential wat of interaction in long-term relationships. This is true when teasing feels loving and comfortable to do by both partners. However, in dominating relationships, teasing can hold emotional abuse in it and being concealed as "I was just teasing you, don't take everything so personally." This will not only make this degrading emotional abuse pass on as teasing, but it will make you feel guilty for ever being offended by it. The controlling partner will not only have succeeded in passing his criticism but will now be able to criticize you even more for having the wrong reaction to his or her teasing. Just keep in mind that you have a right to have your own emotions and express them. Controlling people will make you believe otherwise since this is one of their trademark moves.

Open Relationships

The next type of relationship we are going to briefly present is open relationships. As evidence shows, those relationships are the least probable to end up in a marriage, even though there are people who are married and decided to start an open marriage which is similar to an open relationship. This type of relationship is characterized by a couple who have decided to see other people while they are still involved in the relationship. According to many experts, couples who decide to keep their marriage or

27

relationship open are not that emotionally involved with each other and the two partners do not fill each other on any level which poses many problems.

Non-monogamy is essential for a relationship to be called an open one since both partners are free to engage in romantic and physical relationships with other people and not just one. There are many people who choose this type of relationship or marriage and for this reason, we will analyze briefly the benefits and drawbacks of those relationships for you to know if this is the right path for you. However, keep in mind that those relationships and marriages have a high chance of failing, especially after a while.

The first benefit of an open relationship is that you don't have to be monogamous. Many people do not believe in monogamy and for this reason, they choose to enter an open relationship. They have tried monogamy in the past and they failed so they don't want to adhere to being with one person at a time, however, they still desire a meaningful connection with a partner. When these people are in an open relationship, they will be able to combine both of their desires.

This type of relationship requires honesty about the different people the main couple sees. Both partners are able to find other people to see outside the relationship and all this is based on complete honesty, mutual respect, and open communication.

There may be some feelings for the main partner, but there may also be different needs that other people will be able to fill. This fact doesn't mean that both partners are dishonest about their situation.

Each partner is not in danger of falling into the so-called routine many people are afraid of when they have one stable partner. They will have the constant thrill, excitement, and adventure an open relationship will be able to bring. For example, if the partner is not able to meet the needs of another partner, an open relationship will allow the other person to go after other potential options in order to meet those physical or emotional needs while maintaining the bond he or she has forged with the main partner.

However, in this type of relationship even though it is based on respect and honesty, one of the partners or both partners may develop emotions of jealousy. It is common for people who decide to enter the type of open relationship to feel threatened by all the other people their partner will be involved with. Jealousy is also probable to be developed in monogamous relationships, but in open relationships, the chances are higher due to its nature.

Also, many people make the mistake of thinking that an open relationship will salvage a failing relationship or marriage. It suffices to say that this is completely wrong since an open relationship will almost certainly destroy what is left from both the marriage and relationship. For an open relationship to succeed, there should be less emotion involved and more understanding of the situation.

Open relationships need less emotion involved and more understanding because there is always the danger of one partner falling in love with someone else and decide to end the main relationship. This may leave the other partner vulnerable emotionally and hurt. This will mostly happen for people who only agreed in an open relationship or marriage only because the other partner wished to. If both partners have agreed to enter an open relationship because that was what they truly wanted, then chances are the emotions were not as strong in the first place and the chances of being emotionally hurt are not many, according to experts.

Rebound Relationships

Another type of relationship we will briefly analyze is the rebound relationship. In a rebound relationship, the partners involved have recently experienced a bad breakup and need to make up for the pain. This is another type of relationship that rarely works since its foundations are built on fear of facing the new reality that has been created after a fresh breakup and thus both or one partner is not focusing on the compatibility and dynamic of the new relationship.

According to relationship expert Audrey Hope, "When you're hurting from a past relationship and want to avoid feeling the pain, you jump into another one right away. That's a classic rebound relationship. In a rebound relationship, there is no space and time to process the truth of the past love. The rebounder uses the technique of denial, plus moving on quickly, to stop their feelings. They might be moving so fast, they never stop to learn, or grow, from what was left behind."

Finding a rebound relationship may seem a good solution to alleviate the bad aspects of a breakup, but keep in mind that eventually you will have to face the reality of the situation and rebound relationships may leave you feeling more awful than before. Let us see some classical signs that you are not yet ready to move on to another relationship.

Your phone will tell you everything you need to know since this is one of the main signs, you are not ready to move on to another relationship. Do you catch yourself listening to the special ringtone song, your ex loved? Do you find yourself with a constant need to stop yourself from sending him texts? There is no need to keep telling yourself that you are over him or her since you will be lying to yourself.

According to therapist Kimberly Hershenson, "If you still have your ex's number in your phone, you may be subconsciously holding out hope that they'll reach out again. It may also feel too final to delete their number. Either way, keeping an ex's number handy is a sign you're still hung up on them, and not present in your new relationship."

Make no mistake; this behavior is completely natural after a breakup. However, you are not yet ready to be involved with someone else and you still have issues that need to be dealt with first before you are on the hunt for love again. Besides, it is not fair to the new person you will be seeing if you are out with them and instead of thinking of him or her, you are thinking about whether you should text your ex or not.

Another clue that shows you are not ready to be involved with someone else yet is whether or not you catch yourself addicted to seeing the social media of your ex. You don't believe us? Let us see once again what experts think. According to Kimberly Hershenson, "If you're checking your ex's social media frequently, such as looking at their Facebook, Twitter, and Instagram accounts on a daily, or even weekly basis, it's a sign you're not over them. The need to see what your ex is up to should not be a priority if you are truly ready to move on in your new relationship."

Make no mistake again, this can happen while you are out with a rebound "love" and again this is not fair to the other person unless you have a mutual understanding. Also, it is normal to want to see how your ex is after a breakup, but if this behavior keeps up after a few weeks, keep in mind that this is a desperate and toxic attempt to feel connected to him or her. This will not do you any good since it will keep the hurt alive and will not help you in moving on at all.

Another sign you are entering a rebound relationship and not a serious one because you truly want to is the feeling of falling very quickly, very hard, for someone new that is not your ex. The feeling of having someone to want you, love you, and need you again may be great, but you are not honest with yourself and with the person, you are seeing, so be almost certain that this relationship will not last. Besides, true love needs time to develop; do you really think that love will happen within a few days??

According to relationship expert Audrey Hope, "They have to have the relationship work and may lie and pretend to make this happen. What normally would bother a rebounder is now swept under the rug, and they wear rose-colored glasses. Issues that are serious are just washed away in the new reality of, 'I am going to make this one work, no matter what!' Serious issues in the current relationship will show up later. The rebounder may want to rush to the altar. They could be fueled by pain, or thoughts of revenge, so they may want to get serious much quicker than normal. Watch for this. Ask yourself: 'Why do they want to rush this?"

It suffices to say that do not even think about marrying a rebound partner or if you have doubts that your partner has you as a rebound do not say "yes". This is all rushed and the circumstances will not pose as a solid foundation for a good marriage.

Another sign that you are not yet ready to enter a new relationship and you only seek a rebound is excessive drinking. If you only have a glass of wine in front of the fireplace, this is romantic. However, if on each date you go out, you drink so much to numb the pain, then not only you are not ready for another relationship, but you should watch out for your health. Let us see the word of an expert again to convince you.

According to relationship expert Audrey Hope, "A rebounder may have new issues with substance abuse, to keep the pain under wraps. They may need pills or alcohol, and this problem may grow. Watch for signs of drug or alcohol abuse, that is way more than usual."

With all these signs, it may seem that all rebound relationships are bound to fail. This is certainly the case when the rebounder is in denial and thinks that everything is all rainbows and crystals after a bad breakup. However, not all rebound relationships will fail. Give some time to yourself to grieve for your old relationship. This can be harder to do when you are with someone else. If you really want to make this new relationship work, you first have to work on the unresolved issues you may have from your old relationship. After you have done this, you will be able to mature and have the relationship you deserve.

Added to the above, there are also signs that you are the rebound of the person you are with. Pay attention to these signs so as to avoid any official commitment to that person since it will be doomed to fail if he or she does not change the situation.

The first sign you should look out for is them being smitten with you even though you know them for a very short period of time. We would all love to be the person other people fall in love with immediately due to our good looks and heartwarming personality, but as we have already mentioned, love takes time. If a person you only know for a short period of time tells you that he or she loves you, then chances are they don't because they don't even know you yet. Are they telling you that you are the one for them even though you went out for a few dates in a week? Don't you feel a little bit shocked?

Relationships can move at a slow pace and at the same time at a pretty fast pace. For example, in a matter of weeks, your partner has declared his or her love for you, you are living together, and you spend every moment possible together. However, you start feeling as if you barely know them well enough given the time you spend together and the actual fact that your partner loves you. You feel that despite the fact that you live together; there is no real commitment he or she has towards you or even the other way around. This can also be a sign of you being the rebound of another person, even though it may be a bit difficult to understand.

Another cue that relates to the situation can be that the connection you share makes you feel strangely fulfilling or even completely empty. Your partner is everything you have ever wished for and is so conveniently emotionally free that makes you question if he or she has anything else going on at the moment in their lives. This situation may lead you to the question "Are all this too good to be true?" This is an extremely dangerous situation that is only compared to the feeling of being empty and lonely when you are in the presence of your new partner.

An obvious sign that you are in a rebound relationship that should slow down when there are talks about marriage is that your partner seems bitter over his or her ex. Maybe they insist just too much that they are over their previous relationship or maybe they lash out at an impropriate moment about how wrongfully they were treated by their ex. It suffices to say that there is no marriage, especially in the foreseeable future with this person.

Another sign that your partner is just not over completely their past relationship and you are a rebound is that they are too keen on making their ex jealous by parading you like a doll at places where their ex is. He or she could also have a very satisfying and evil look in their eyes when they post cute couple selfies of the two of you. Think of your partner as the villain in a movie. Both creepy and with no honest intentions.

If your partner still keeps a large number of pictures with his or her ex around the house or tends to talk with a longing look about their past relationship, then your partner is still into this previous relationship and no, you will not be able to fix them. Getting over an ex is a personal process and no person should go through the usually painful process of helping someone romantically to get over a past relationship. If you are not able to have fun with that person because they always talk about their ex, leave quickly.

When your partner wants to act as if you are a long term couple while you have just started dating, then this is not a common behavior and may indicate that your partner has some unresolved issues with his or her past relationship. They want to talk to you as if you have known each other for years and force relationship jokes only the two of you should know. Maybe your partner has already decided which side of your bd is your and which side is his. They expressed their desire to roam around the house in sweats and go to various errands together instead of doing things new couples do. Your partner has already set a relationship routine and this routine is the one he was used to with his ex-partner.

Two other cues that show you are in a rebound relationship are the fact that you and your partner do not have much in common and your partner's interest changes out of the blue between hot and cold cues. In the first case, you are just watching movies and having a lot of sex, because your partner possibly needs to forget the pain and feel some human contact and you want to have a nice time with your partner, and in the second case, your partner seems obsessed with you one moment and in another moment he or she is placing a cold distance between the two of you. This sudden mood change could be a remnant of a recent breakup because they don't know what they truly want.

Also, if you notice that your partner doesn't know what to tell you when you ask him or her to talk about themselves, for example about their hobbies, it may because they are not over their last breakup. After you break up with someone, especially if the relationship was long, you may feel that certain parts of your life before the relationship have changed completely when this part vanishes. If your partner isn't able to tell you much about themselves other than talk about their past relationship then they need time to heal and find themselves again without the presence of their ex.

Last but not least you may feel as if your partner compares you to his or her ex and you feel as if your partner just picked you up out of a lot of other choices. Int he first case, your partner may tell you suddenly how much better you are when compared to his or her ex. This is not truly a compliment since it is a sign that they still think about them. In the second case, if this is how your partner makes you feel, it is time to leave the relationship as soon as possible because he or she will not love you as you deserve.

Compatible Relationships

The last type of relationship we are going to briefly analyze is the one who will almost certainly lead to a happy and solid marriage. This relationship type is the truly compatible relationship. This is a healthy relationship between two people that love, understand, and trust each other. They have worked hard to build the relationship by making sacrifices for each other and managed to create effective communication as well as share a mutual respect for their partner. Compatible partners share certain traits that help them make their relationship compatible too. Let us take a look at these traits.

The first thing two compatible people never do is to question the love they feel in their relationship. Each partner knows they love the other and there have no doubts about how much they know their partner or how much they love them. They feel happy and secure in their relationship, even if one or both partners tend to worry much by nature. They never feel inclined to question the feelings of the other partner since they have managed to create a solid relationship.

Compatible people know stuff about each other that no other person knows, except maybe the parents of the partners. They know every embarrassing story to personal details about their whole lives. By sharing their secrets and inner desires, goals, and events they were able to know how compatible they truly are with their partner. They know how important honesty is in a relationship and they were not forced to share those details. They wanted to share those secrets with their partner and showed to him or her how invested and serious they are in their relationship.

Also, they respect each other too much to try and change their partner as an individual. There are certain things that they may not like, but to them, they seem minuscule since they believe there are more important things to worry about than the way a partner dresses or sleeps. Each partner loves the other and they compromise to such things. It is true that if you want to change the personality of your partner, you are not truly compatible because this means that there are many things you don't like about him or her.

Compatible people know how important it is to spend some time alone for the relationship. When two people are involved in a great relationship that fulfils their needs, it may be hard to be away. However, if this relationship is built to last, it is important to spend some time alone and away from your partner. Enjoy some time with your friends and family or even by indulging in your hobbies. Compatible people still understand the important meaning of alone time since they are still separate individuals with different friends and family members.

As we have mentioned, having your own hobbies is important as well as interests, but compatible partners still try to spend some time together along with their shared interests and hobbies by indulging in things they enjoy. Long term relationships that lead to a solid marriage are maintained in a large part by shared interests for the couple to fight less and spend a joyful time together.

All these do not mean that compatible people do not fight. Not only do they fight but they are not afraid to do so too. They know that disagreements will not change the way they feel about each other and that they are entitled to express their feelings when they disagree with something that their partner says or does. In turn, they know that their partner will listen to them and take them seriously. If the disagreement is not resolved by one partner agreeing with the opinion of the other, they realize that this is okay too. They are two different people who will find a way to solve a problem when the need arises.

Serious problems do not scare people who are compatible with each other. Whether they are about money, where they will leave together, or religion, they will feel certain that they will be solved since they are both willing to compromise and are compatible. In long term relationships as well as in solid marriages, it is essential to be able to work together until a decision is made that both partners are happy with. It suffices to say that in order for both partners to be happy, they need to compromise, but never in a way that the needs of one person will be completely overlooked.

Another sign of people who are compatible with each other is that each partner inspires the other to be a better person. Although you may have heard his a million times, people who fit together, work together to becoming the better version of themselves. They inspire each other to move forward. This could be as simple as learning how to cook or something more serious such as working hard to get the promotion you so much deserve at work. In other words, you will know that your partner always has your back and supports you. Of course, your partner should feel the same way this in return.

One important thing that shows how truly compatible are two people is to be able to imagine their future together. This will also set a solid foundation for your potential marriage and it will make both partners sure of its success. Two people should be on the same page when they talk about the future. If your interests are not completely the same, don't worry much about it. For example, you may want to get married and have children and your partner wants to travel. When these are your differences rest assured because you will be able to do both. However, if you or your partner does not wish to talk about a common future, it may be a serious indicator that you need different things from your relationship and life in general.

There are many people that feel as if they shouldn't be themselves around their partner because they will not like what they see and leave them. They take on a different personality that fits the standards of the partner all the while suppressing their true personality and ending up being a totally different person. This is not the case with truly compatible people that have built a solid relationship that will lead to a solid marriage. A person should be able to truly be themselves whenever they are around their partner.

They should be allowed to express their anger, happiness, sadness, or worries to their partner as well as every other emotion they experience without having to worry about the reaction of their partner. If you feel that you should hide your personality to fit the standards of your partner, then you should talk to your partner about this and if it gets you nowhere, end the relationship.

Another sign of truly compatible partners is the effort they put to get along with the family of the other. If you are truly getting along with the family of your partner, then this is great, but this is not always the case. Loving your partner does not necessarily guarantee that you will get along with your partner's family. However, you put some effort to get along with your partner's family. Keep in mind that everyone has a family and when you marry this person, he or she will not abandon their family.

In order for a long term relationship and eventually, for a marriage to be solid, the spark must be kept alive. There many cases of married couples that get lost in work, children, and the many other responsibilities they have, but those should not be left to affect the relationship and let it die. Even though those responsibilities should not be neglected, there is always time to spend with your partner and make him or her feel important. It is always important to make an effort for your partner and thus the relationship.

After being married for a long time those responsibilities may make you or your partner t feel neglected and unhappy. People who are compatible know that they should not give up and fall into a constant routine that leads to neglect. They will show their partners that they care and feel appreciated. You should be excited about your partner and show him off to your friends and family. You should of course not be embarrassed about him or her.

Every marriage starts off from a relationship and when the relationship is not built on solid foundations, and then the marriage will crumble. Imagine having built a house out of cards, with the first soft wind it will collapse and in order for it to be repaired, it will take much more time and effort than many people can handle. In most cases, no one will want to build another house out of cards but will turn to find another, more solid house to live the rest of their lives in. This is the reason why you should first build a solid relationship before you move on to be married. In other words, a solid relationship will most probably give you a solid marriage.

Chapter 2: The Different Types of Men

We have talked about the different types of relationships in order for you to understand in which situation you are at the moment, as well as the necessary steps you need to take to make things better or leave the relationship altogether before it develops into a marriage proposal and then in divorce. However, besides building a solid relationship that is the first step in having a solid marriage, you need to know the kind of person you have by your side. Experts through research and experience have helped us in identifying the different types of men that exist along with their certain characteristics and behaviors.

We will present you with the most common types so as for you to be able to identify the different types your man belongs to and what to expect from him. However, keep in mind that each person is different and those types are only used as a guide of what you should generally expect. Also, it is common for men to have characteristics of different types. All in all, you know your man better and this will guide you through in realizing if you are compatible with each type of man and which one fulfills your needs more. Marriage symbolized our intent to live with someone forever and the type of person we are with plays an essential role in fulfilling this intent. Last but not least, we will also delve further into the type of the narcissist since relationships with this type of man are most dangerous and manipulative. They rarely lead to marriage and if they do, they are rarely happy ones.

The Selfish Man

The first type of man we will analyze is the selfish man. Generally, selfish men will always ask and rarely, if ever, give back anything in return. He will not give you his jacket when you are cold and will not have your back unless it has something to do with him. Selfish people only worry about themselves and have little regard for others. Usually, selfish men are not aware they are being this way and actually think of themselves as nice people who care about making themselves happy more than anything else.

According to F. Diane Barth in Psychology Today, you will see two trademark characteristics of selfish people, "Being concerned excessively or exclusively with oneself; Having no regard for the needs or feelings of others."

Selfish men don't care to place themselves in the shoes of other people and even if they do, they will not care enough to do anything about the things that concern you. If you constantly communicate your needs to a selfish man and he is doing nothing about it or only assures you that everything will be better without actually doing anything about it, then be certain that he cares only about himself. this is often the reason why you should pay attention more to the action of the person you are with rather than words. Remember, sometimes, actions speak louder than words.

When you are in the middle of an argument and you support your beliefs and views of the matter you are arguing with, he will most probably leave and refuse to deal with you until you see things from his perspective or generally change your mind. This is a form of controlling behavior and cam even be considered as emotional abuse, depending on the situation and the matter you are arguing with.

This stance is considered as abusive because he will make you less decisive about voicing your beliefs and in order to avoid confrontation, you may even adhere to his own demands and needs. This will result in changing the dynamic of the relationship and make it less equal by stripping it of its give and take nature. By refusing to discuss and get into an argument with the intent of compromise, in the end, this man presents a cruel behavior that it will be difficult to overcome unless it suits him.

Also, if you start having second thoughts about your behavior towards him such as thinking that you are indeed being unreasonable with him, then this is a sign of him controlling you. When a person is in a relationship with a partner who is selfish, the one who is doubting their decisions is not the selfish partner, but the normal one to the extent that the other person becomes a doormat for the selfish partner. The obvious truth of the matter is that you are not unreasonable for wanting respect. Actually, you shouldn't just want respect, but also demand it. Everyone needs their partner to take their needs and feelings into consideration and work together so as to create a relationship that will have you both feeling secure and calm.

Also, a selfish man will keep doing things that he knows are making you uncomfortable. This could either mean that he is denying giving you affection and attention or that he keeps flirting with other women. He may keep standing you up on scheduled dates or not keep his promises. In order for a relationship to be healthy, each partner should take into consideration the feelings of the other and not blatantly disregard them as if they mean nothing. If this is the case, then it should be better to get out of this relationship before things turn serious.

Many of these men are struggling with maintaining serious relationships and they often do not know why this is the case. One obvious reason is that relationships demand from you to be able to think of your partner, sometimes even more than you think of yourself and this is something they are not able to do or they do not even try to do it. Think of it this way, a selfish man does not need a partner, he needs a nanny.

The Perfect Gentleman

The next type we will analyze is the perfect gentleman. He is the man who firmly believes that chivalry is not yet dead. He has great manners and will always keep the door open for you. He will make the perfect boyfriend and husband because he knows how to treat people. He will take your needs into consideration as long as you do the same. Reciprocity is a virtue and this type of man believes in all the virtues of good behavior.

One important trait of a gentleman is his punctuality. A true gentleman will never make you wait and for this reason, he is always on time and sometimes, he is even earlier than the time you were supposed to meet. This is his way of showing his respect for you and certainly, this is an important trait. People often tend to get very frustrated when they are waiting for others especially on a date and who could blame them? Unless there is a good reason when we are being stood up because our date had to change into a new pair of shoes sets off the wrong vibe.

Anyway, you will not have to deal with these difficulties when you are with the gentleman type. The respect he is showing you is a must in a serious relationship and if he is being respectful of such seemingly simple things, then you should certainly expect respect on every level of the relationship. In the rare situations that he is late, he will call you to inform you as soon as possible.

51

A gentleman will always open doors for you, including car doors. Do not mistake this trait as him showing you that you are unable to open a door for yourself. On the contrary, he lets you lead the way. He lets you be the first one to move and he will follow. This can be considered as another sign of showing his respect for you.

He respects you enough to not overshadow you and this is why he will also always walk on the curbside whenever you are walking together. On the occasions you are both walking down the street, a gentleman will always be on the curb side so as to not place you in any harm. He is not trying to impose or think of you as a weak person. He is only looking out for your well being by endangering his own life.

When a gentleman is interested in someone, he will not wait three days to call, but he will call to ask this person out to dinner, make the reservations for himself and treat this person with the utmost care. Not to mention he will make sure that you will arrive home safe and sound. If he is interested in a person he will let them know and even if he isn't, he will be polite about it. He will let the other person know gently that he is not interested so as to not waste both their time since the relationship between them will not work.

Also, a gentleman will offer you his jacket when you are cold to make sure you will not get sick and stay as warm as possible. He will also assist you when you will sit by pulling your chair for you before he takes a seat for himself. He will make sure you are comfortable before he attends to his own comfort and needs. One of the first things you will notice about a gentleman is that he will always give up his seat for other people.

For example, he will not hesitate for even a moment to offer his seat to the pregnant women, the handicapped, the elderly or anyone who is in need. This is again a sign of respect and a sign that he will sacrifice his own comfort for those who need it more than him. A gentleman will not only shower you with respect but other people too. This is the main reason why he knows the true meaning of the word.

A gentleman is always informed about the things that happen in this world since he will be keen on reading books and newspapers. He will have an opinion on almost everything, from a small gathering that is taking place to world events and he will express this opinion when he is asked about it. He understands that his opinions are not facts and will not get into a fight with anyone that disagrees with him.

The most important thing for you to understand here is that a gentleman will not need to feel validated by others in order to prove his manhood. His opinions are his own, everyone is welcome to disagree with him and even engage in a constructive conversation that will lead to intelligent debate.

Another trademark sign of a gentleman is that he adheres to the basic courtesy of not eating first. He will wait for everyone to start eating before he starts to eat too as a sign of respect. Another sign of his respect for you is shown when he is offering his hand or arm for you to hold so as to ensure your stability. Be it when you walk down the stairs or down the street, a gentleman will always do this to show you how special you are.

A gentleman is still a man and will want to get the person he is interested in to be sexually intimate with him, but he wants first to win over the person's mind before he moves on to other things. However, if his partner takes advantage of his kindness and thoughtfulness, he will not hesitate to leave the relationship because he doesn't have to be a doormat for anyone. His self-esteem and confidence are established and he knows his worth as a person. He demands the same respect to be given to him as he gives to others.

A gentleman's manners are so well developed that he will expertly know when to follow etiquette. He will know when he will need to eat with his hands when he is for example at a BBQ and he will certainly know when he needs to use the napkin and eat with more class, for example, when he is in a restaurant for a date whether it is a professional one or a personal one. Another testament that shows his manners are impeccable is the fact that he is never obnoxious or rude to others. He knows that the right way to show his accomplishments is not by bragging about them. He lets his actions speak for themselves and will never be rude to anyone, even those who are rude to him. He can defend himself without being crude and knows that yelling or cursing in public will not make him more of a man.

The one thing that will make you understand a gentleman more than anything else is that he is not a good boy or a bad boy. He is not even considered as a boy at all. He is a real man who is not looking for someone to pass his time with. He is looking for someone that will share his beliefs and not judge him about them or even try to change him. He is also looking for someone that will be able to teach him more things about himself and the world around him along the way. He values intelligence as much as he values appearance, even if not more. He is willing to work in a relationship as long as the person he is with is willing to do the same.

He will be attentive and when he is out with a person, he will offer them his undivided attention. This includes not touching his phone to scroll down the social media pages whenever you are talking to him. He will be an active listener and will not only pretend to listen to you. He will not share the details of your relationship and will never brag about getting you into bed with him. He will be true to his word and will not make excuses if things did not go as planned. A gentleman understands that healthy relationships are built on trust and for this reason; he will do everything in his power to never let you down.

He also knows that secrets are secrets and will not blab about something, someone has told him in confidence. He will tell you the truth even if it hurts because this is a matter of integrity for him and this is another trait he values. He is a protector and will always help you with household chores or other issues you will need a shoulder to rely on.

This type of man seems too good to be true, but he exists. Being married to him will lead to a solid marriage because he will be open to forge a strong communication system and compromise in a way that both sides are satisfied as long as his partner does not take advantage of his caring nature.

The Alpha Male

The next type of men we are going to present is the alpha male. In its core, the term "alpha male" refers to the real man. Confident but not arrogant, decisive and sometimes gentle. Powerful but calm. Being an alpha male doesn't have to do with being rich, how many women you have slept with, how much your car costs or how big your body is. Sure there are alpha males who look like bodybuilders and rich as well as charming enough, but this is not always the case.

Essentially being an alpha male requires you to be in control of your own life. It has to do with leading yourself and the people you love to a better future. An alpha male knows which ae his values and will always adhere to them. This male has a vision and will do anything within his power to make it happen. That man is the leader other people look up to for motivation and advice, often with jealousy. He is the man most women want exactly.

One of the main traits of the alpha male is that he is persistent and will not give up the fight of attaining his goals no matter how hard they are. He will be the last man standing and he will fall fighting since he is a born leader and a fighter. For this reason, he will be able to defend his family and himself. He will not accept an insulting word about those he loves and he will stand up for them when the occasion calls for it.

He is in great physical shape, but it doesn't necessarily mean that he is a bodybuilder. He knows the benefits of living a healthy life and he adheres to this way of life. He believes in his looks and that women are attracted to him even though he may not be as handsome as a model. He is very confident and masculine because he knows his strengths and that insecurity makes him weak and will never get him anything important in life.

He keeps his patience and composure when he is under pressure because he has realized and developed the skill of getting through difficult situations. For this reason, he will be constantly motivated to achieve whatever it is he wants to achieve in his life. This doesn't necessarily translate to succeeding the first time he will try anything. However, if he fails, he will not give up trying and every failure will be a lesson to him on what he has to learn to do better next time.

Another important trait of the alpha male is his courage. He may be afraid, but rather than letting fear control him, he accepts it and is moving forward by facing and grabbing each opportunity that presents itself. This is why he is also a leader. He may not be perfect since he knows that no one is, but he accepts the fact that someone has to lead be it on a professional level or a personal one. When the need arises he will take up the task due to his courageous nature.

Also, he knows that some people may not like him. A person cannot be liked by everyone. However, he expects them to respect him and is not hoping or trying to be liked. He knows the importance of showing his true colors and being honest about his personality. This is also why the people that stick with him will be his true friends and family. They have accepted him for who he is and there is no reason to show another personality when he is around them.

He is not ashamed of making mistakes since he knows that all people make mistakes and recognizes them as an opportunity to learn and grow as a person. He is improving though his mistakes and thus he is able to take up more challenges when he perfects his past failures. He is always evolving according to his standards, values, and the things he is passionate about.

An alpha male has a great sense of humor and can make people hang to his every word. He is great at telling stories and narrating experiences. Often the experiences of an alpha male are so educational that people feel drawn to learn from him and always seek him up for advice. He knows the different ways he can catch the attention of a group of people and never let them feel bored when in his presence. This makes people want to be like him.

Other men will either respect him or be jealous of him and wonder how they can be like the alpha male. An alpha male will make his own way through life by creating his own future rather than hope for life opportunities to present themselves while he sits around doing nothing. He learns everything he can and will even go as far as to demand great things to happen to him. He is persistent and on this part of life, persistence will be the key to his success as long as he is able to handle the various obstacles and he is because the alpha male faces life head-on.

An alpha male will be able to make fun of himself and laugh at his expense. This essentially means that other people will not be able to make fun of him, in a way that makes them feel they managed to bring him down so as to make themselves look better. An alpha male will join in any joke that is made at his expense.

He knows how to indulge in self-sarcasm and this is a great skill that few people have.

He understands there is no reason to be insulted by the opinion others have of him since the only opinion that matters to him is his own and that of the people he cares about. A fun fact is that no one can make better fun of the alpha male than he can. So, chances are people will laugh at the jokes he makes of himself rather than the jokes others make about him.

An alpha male is also humble. He will never brag about his accomplishments because he wants to succeed for his own personal reasons that do not include him bragging to everyone he knows about his successes. He wants to succeed in life because this is his way of being fulfilled and the only way he could provide for himself and his family, not because he wants to look successful in the eyes of strangers and acquaintances. He will never let himself get carried away by fame and fortune and forget his value and everything he believes in.

Added to the above, an alpha male is educated and knows many things that are useful to his life. This doesn't necessarily mean that he has a dree but is most certainly means that he has a thirst to learn and learn more things every day. This thirst for knowledge will make him the perfect companion for every person of every social or economic standing. He will be an active participant in a conversation with a businessman, a historian, a person who loves sports, or even a preacher.

When an alpha male is talking, every word he says, counts. He knows that words have value and he will never speak just to hear himself talking and admire the way he says everything. He chooses his words with care and is respectful of the power words have. He knows that by talking too much he risks the boredom of everyone in the room or just his companion and also it will most probably make him look like an arrogant man who is too full of himself. He knows that words are able to hurt a person and this is the reason why he speaks only when he has something to contribute to the conversations, something of value to say.

An alpha male has a purpose that defines his life. When he succeeds this purpose, he will make a new one. He will not let his life pass before his eyes trying to find himself. He will find himself along the way. He sees every day as a new opportunity that will bring him closer to his goal. For this reason, he is working hard since he realizes that nothing great will be accomplished without a purpose and hard word.

Also, he realizes that there are certain things that he will not be able to control. He is going to control the things he can, but for those, he is not able to keep under his supervision, he will not worry. He knows that he has to work today and not be worried about tomorrow. He knows exactly who he is as well as the values that govern his life. He will try anything in his power to never stray from those values, but he realizes that a person should "never say never". He will stand up for what he believes in and even if he all alone, he will still stand up for what he believes is right.

The alpha male will not go out of his way to please everyone since he isn't a people pleaser. H will not let anyone control his life since he is his own person. Even though he will worship the ground his partner will walk on, he will make certain he will pick the right partner who will not take advantage of this behavior. He will most certainly not be with a jealous or controlling woman since he will completely trust his partner and expects the same from them.

When an alpha male starts something he will not abandon it halfway. He is stubborn and he will see everything through until the end. He will not let anyone stop him from doing whatever he thinks needs to be done, but this doesn't mean that he will not listen to other people's opinions. He knows that he is not perfect and can be stubborn, so he is open to learning from other people that are always better than him. He will not endanger the accomplishments he worked so hard to achieve by listening to someone who had not managed to do whatever he did.

The secret for most alpha males being this way is that they are not trying to be one. Being an alpha male is more of a mindset than physical characteristics or a guide through which there are certain rules for other men to follow. He is interested in living a full life and can be awed by the world around him. He wants to be the best man he can be and cares about others as well as respects them. He is not afraid to work hard since he understands this is the only way he will achieve all the goals he has and will set throughout life.

An alpha male would be another perfect choice for marriage, especially if you are his one and only. He will be eager to fix any problems that may arise throughout your lives together since he is great at solving problems and will always take your needs and opinion into consideration. He will be a protector and a provider and he will never cage you down since he knows that you are your own person. He will respect you and will expect similar behavior from you. Respect the alpha male and never try to dictate his life because this is when the real problems will start.

The Mama's Boy

The next type of man we are going to present to you is the mama's boy. Those men have let for some reason their mothers play an extremely important role in their dating life. We are not talking about letting her express a simple opinion. No. A mama's boy will always choose their mother over you to the extent that he will let her insult you without standing up for you and will refuse to marry you if his mother does not approve of you.

If you are one of the lucky ones and his mother likes you, rest assured that a person who is able to love his mom so much will most probably respect and love their partner this much too. I don't think we should tell you that if his mother is not that into you, you are in for a ride. Let us some of the main characteristics of a mama's boy to further understand this type of man and if you want to marry a person like this or not.

To start with this man could never survive living on his own. While this can be true for most bachelors, it really isn't. When people live on their own they are forced to learn how to at least boil an egg and use the dishwasher. Unless of course, he is rich, so they are able to order takeout food. A mama's boy is not able to wash his own clothes, he does not know how to work with a dishwasher and the foods he eats are prepared in a microwave. If you are wondering where he is washing his clothes, search no more. It will be at his parent's house since most of his days are spend there to eat a decent meal. Obviously, those skills have not been mastered yet because his mother is doing everything for him. Why does this guy even own his own apartment?

Another sign that your man is a mama's boy is when he has to ask her about everything he makes a decision on. While it is normal for a person, no matter what age he or she is, to get the opinion of their parents, it is not normal for someone to ask his mother which color of blouse he should wear for his date with you. This is probably based on this man's belief that his mother cannot do anything wrong. Everything she believes is correct and is the wisest woman in this world. He will never disagree with her even when they are all alone. His mother could say that the universe does not exist and he would believe her as well as stand up for her when everyone else was shocked.

Another sign that your partner is a mama's boy is that his mother knows about everything that is happening between the two of you. Who is he going to call first when you have a fight? His mother. She may even know more about the emotions of her son than you do, not because of motherly intuition but because he tells her more about his feelings that have to do about your relationship than you, the actual person who is involved in this relationship or marriage.

Everyone likes it when their mother pampers them a little when they come home to visit. We feel like children again, but we do not start acting like ones. A line must be drawn when his mother starts to cut his dinner down for him and a mama's boy will rarely draw this line. Also, as adults, we have developed a personal style. Our mothers may not agree with our choice, but we rarely listen. Do not be shocked if you see your man changing clothes since his mother doesn't like them even if you bought them for him.

You may not have to worry about this type of man comparing you to his ex, but you will have to worry about him comparing you to his mother. She is the only woman, he will ever compare his partners to and that includes you too. You will probably see him being critical of the way you cook and compare it to the cooking methods of his mother or expecting of you to have the same or similar professional career and parenting methods. It suffices to say that this trait should be cut down and be dealt with as soon as possible. This may also stem from the fact that he is spoiled and any need or responsibility he has is transferred to his mother. He knows that his mother has spoiled him and e is taking advantage of it. He is so spoiled, you are not even sure if he has managed to pay a bill alone in his life.

Another characteristic of this type of man is when his mother is showing up without warning any of you first. Let us take the worst-case scenario of you being in an intimate situation and his mom shows up unannounced because she missed her son whom she had seen the day before. Of course, this has happened because she was allowed to do so by her son who will never tell his mother to ask before she visits him. He will never be completely independent of her and she will even cook at your place all the while making little snide "jokes" of how her son must be starving without her magic cooking skills.

Also, he will never believe something unless his mother tells him that it is alright to do so. For example, you may have decided to cook together or book a vacation. On both occasions, if the process is not exactly the same as his mother has done it, then it is not the right way. There is no need to mention more serious matter such as buying a new house to live or investments. If his mother does not approve of the hour and the neighborhood, then you can be certain that you are not going to live there. Even if this is your dream house. We are so sorry to be the bearer of bad news.

Do not think for a moment that you will get off the hook when you move in with this type of guy. If you have managed to get him to buy the house you want, good for you, or you gave in and decided to live in the house that has been approved first by his mother, she will try to control your life too since she will think that she will have a say on how you decorate it. You either have to be the bad guy and refuse or let her do what she wants to an extent. Do not assume that this type of man will tell his mother no.

Whatever the matter is, be it buying new furniture or where to go on vacation on holidays, his mother will always have the final say. Even if you succeed in making him see your point and even agree with you, all it will take is one call from his mother to bring you back to square one. Do not be surprised if your vacation includes his parents too because his mother always wanted to visit Paris. He is so stubborn that he will not accept no for an answer. He is so used to getting his own way around when he was with his mother that he will try to continue this behavior with you too. If you are patient enough, you may make him understand why it is important to compromise, but it will really take a long time.

Also, do not expect to be able to make jokes about his mother, even innocent ones. The mother of this type of man is his world and he will never accept any joke that is made at her dispense. Even if you do one, he will not be able to let it go and it may turn out to be a huge fight between the two of you. And don't be too surprised if you haven't heard from him almost all day and when you return home he tells you he has been extremely busy. Chances are that if you look at his messages, he wasn't too busy to start a whole texting conversation with his mother. Don't even bother to point this out to him, he will just tell you that this doesn't count because it was his mom.

This type of man will lack motivation since he had everything handed to him from his mother for his whole life. He will not understand or will certainly struggle to realize how important it is to work hard in order to succeed in life. However, this is not necessarily his fault because he was raised this way and he is paying now for the mistakes both his parents did.

He was never allowed or taught how to work hard and seek more of his life than a mediocre job that will pay his bills, even if that because his mother will always be there to give him as much money as he needs. On the other hand, this is not your fault either, so the best course of action for you is to encourage him and support him in this newfound path. Make him understand that in order to succeed in life and to keep your relationship he must put some effort if not a lot of it to make something out of his life just as you do.

Also, when he is sick expect him to act like a baby. No matter how much you try to make him feel better, you will always do something wrong. Why? Because his mother was doing it better and not like you. For this reason, expect his mother to come and take care of him the right way. She will make her magic soup and also complain about the dust on the furniture and how this is not helping her son get better.

Being with this type of man may seem like a great challenge but keep in mind that if you pass the problems that may occur with his mother, this man will certainly know how to treat women and is actually a very kind soul. Being married to this man will have many benefits and it will be perfect if you manage to solve the problem his relationship with his mother poses.

The Serial Cheater

The next type of man we are going to take a brief look at is the serial cheater. It is a true fact that infidelity places the most serious relationships and marriages in danger since we all make mistakes. However, one mistake by a person who feels extremely sorry and is a wreck by making this awful choice is something completely different than being someone who indulges in affairs for years and cheating is his sport and hobby. There are some people that are simply unable to be monogamous and for this reason, they are called serial cheaters, cheating is their specific trait.

According to psychologist Dr. Ildiko Tabori, «There are psychological characteristics that are more prevalent and revealing about the personality traits of people who cheat." We will present you with some common traits of serial cheaters because infidelity is one of the most common reasons relationships and marriages are destroyed.

The first trait of a serial cheater is that they get easily bored when they are in long-term relationships. To this type of man, monogamy is compared to a strict diet, with the only difference that no piece of chocolate actually hurts a people's emotions by making them feel betrayed. They always need the thrill that comes from the novelty that stems from being with someone new.

There is nothing you can do to make yourself appear as someone new and you shouldn't even try to. These men will never make good boyfriends let alone good husbands.

According to Dr. Tabori, "People who cheat prefer to ride an emotional roller coaster rather than find joy in emotional stability. They get an adrenaline rush from the figurative bumps and bruises that cause strife and turmoil with their significant other and their second significant other because it leads to the intoxication of making up again and again."

Another characteristic of a serial cheater is that he never makes any promises and he never will openly confess his feelings towards you if there are any. They will never engage in serious conversations that have to do with a joint future and even if they do it will be very vague and without any details. According to Kevin Darné, "Serious discussions usually lead to making promises, giving reassurances, setting expectations, emotional investment, and developing a deeper commitment. Serial cheaters prefer to have their partner assume what he or she feels instead of having to openly express and confirm those feelings or their status. This allows them a certain deniability if they're ever caught cheating since they can say, 'We never said we were exclusive."

Also, most serial cheaters are afraid of being alone, whether you want to believe it or not. They find a second partner and use this relationship as some sort of security blanket that will protect them against emotional and physical loneliness. However, this method is not working since their affair will be revealed and they will surely lose their main relationship and most probably their security blanket too. This will not prevent them from doing this again since their fear will prevail wit time and most of these men are not able to admit they are afraid and have a problem.

Added to this, serial cheaters will not change, but will get extremely opportunistic. They will not change, but may be good for a while until you are assured that something like this will not happen again. When you let your guard down and trust him again, this is when he will strike again. According to Joshua Forman, a matrimonial attorney at Chemtob Moss & Forman, "Some people do change, but as a whole, if someone cheated on you before you got married, a leopard doesn't change their spots. They might get good for a couple months, but it's not the kind of thing that changes. The personality traits of someone who is dishonest in work or in other areas spills over into personal life."

Serial cheaters are more common among men who are in a position of power since they can be extremely calculating on when it is the perfect opportunity for them to make the same mistake again and again. More specifically, Dr. Tabori says, "One is more likely to cheat when opportunity arises, not simply when they are away from their significant other, but when the opportunity to prey upon a potential mate presents itself. People who cheat will look for opportunities where the potential mate may be in a vulnerable state, such as after a break-up or divorce. When the preyed-upon is in a more vulnerable state, they are more likely to be open to and engage in the cheating behavior because they miss the feeling of being loved and are not emotionally grounded enough yet to set secure boundaries."

Another sign that a man is a serial cheater is his constant admission that infidelity is not that serious since everyone cheats. Generally, he will try to justify this action and you should get away from this person since anyone who thinks that infidelity in a marriage is something common, he is bound to do it himself. Also, a serial cheater will not care about what you do where you are, mainly because they think that you shouldn't care too. They will not ask you about your day because they do not want you to ask about theirs too. According to Kevin Darné, "If your cell phone went dead and you were unable to contact them until the following day it might surprise you to find your date hadn't attempted to reach you. They avoid asking you a lot of questions because they don't want you asking them a lot of questions. Trusting someone does not mean you do not get to ask them questions. Trusting someone means you believe they will give you honest answers to your questions."

Serial cheaters know that their behavior is hurtful and disrespectful towards the person they are with. However, they are not willing to change their ways because they don't want to do it. They lack in self-control or discipline and for this reason, they will most probably never change. It goes without saying that these men will never be husband material and you will never be able to have a solid marriage with them.

The Narcissist

The next type of man we are going to present is the narcissistic man who is never going to be able to have a functional, healthy relationship let alone create a solid marriage. A true narcissist suffers from narcissistic personality disorder (NPD) which is a personality disorder where people have a distorted and extravagant opinion of themselves. They have an immense need for attention and admiration from other people and when they are not praised, people with narcissistic personality disorder will be very disappointed and unhappy.

This personality disorder is characterized by:

  ✓ a feeling of them being very important persons
  ✓ a need for excessive admiration and attention
  ✓ absence of empathy for other people
  ✓ almost always they have troubled relationships

For a person to be considered as a narcissist the following criteria should be met:

- ✓ extreme sense of self-importance
- ✓ focus on fantasies that involve unlimited success, power, brilliance, beauty, or ideal love
- ✓ a sense that they are unique and special so they can be only understood by other special people with high status and those are the only ones they should hang out with
- ✓ need for excessive admiration
- ✓ sense of entitlement
- ✓ interpersonally exploitative behavior
- ✓ lack of empathy
- ✓ jealousy of others or a belief that others are envious of them
- ✓ the appearance of arrogant and haughty behaviors or attitudes

The above are some criteria experts have set in order for people to be able to recognize narcissists. However, when you are involved in a romantic relationship with one it may be difficult to determine a narcissist. Besides, a person who is dating this type of man never wonders if they actually suffer from a particular personality disorder, but if the behavior of their partner is appropriate and healthy for a long-term relationship.

At first, narcissists will appear as extremely charming men who will make all your fairy tale dreams come true. They will text you immediately or tell you they love you too soon, something that experts have named "love bombing". They will confess and admire how smart you are and how great you are together even though you have only started to go out. According to Nedra Glover Tawwab, who is the founder of Kaleidoscope Counseling, "Narcissists think that they deserve to be with other people who are special, and that special people are the only ones who can appreciate them fully."

However, the moment you do something that disappoints them, you will experience a completely different person. You will have no idea what you have done, but be certain that your wrongdoing will have nothing to do with you and everything to do with your narcissistic partner beliefs. Be careful because if you think that your partner tells you too soon how strongly he feels about you, it probably is. According to licensed therapist Rebecca Weiler, LMHC, "If you think it's too early for them to really love you, it probably is. Or if you feel like they don't know enough about you to actually love you, they probably don't."

Another trait of this type of man is their constant bragging about how great they are and about their accomplishments, which will not always be as great as they sound. They will tend to enrich their skills and successes in order to gain the, much needed to them, attention and admiration of other people. More specifically, according to psychotherapist Jacklyn Krol, of Mind Rejuvenation Therapy, "Narcissists love to constantly talk about their own accomplishments and achievements with grandiose. They do this because they feel better and smarter than everyone else, and also because it helps them create an appearance of being self-assured."

Also, they will never listen to you since they will either be too busy talking about themselves or think of the additional lies he will tell you. Your partner will keep talking about themselves and will not start a conversation about you or interrupt you when you start talking about yourself. Do you see them asking follow up questions to keep the conversation about yourself going? Do they seem interested to learn more things about you? Or do they make everything you say about them?

This type of man usually comes off as strong and self-confident, but the opposite is true. They are insecure and feel good only when you compliment them. Most people who have this personality disorder lack self-esteem. This is also the reason why they need attention and admiration so much. According to Shirin Peykar, LMFT, "Narcissists use other people, people who are typically highly empathic, to supply their sense of self-worth, and make them feel powerful. But because of their low self-esteem, their egos can be slighted very easily, which increases their need for compliments."

Due to this lack of self-confidense, narcissist men will make confident people pay about this skill by being extremely difficult to live with. Confident people do nt rely on anyone to understand what they are worth, they will feel good about themselves no matter who likes them or not. To put it in the words of According to Shirin Peykar, "The main difference between folks who are confident and those with NPD is that narcissists need others to lift them up, and lift themselves up only by putting others down. Two things people with high self-confidence do not do."

Another trait of this type of man is their lack of empathy. They are not able to feel the emotions of another person or even understand it and be supportive. Narcissists just don't do feelings; they only care for you to admire them. Your partner will not care that you had a bad day or fought with your parents. They will be bored when you express your emotions or talk about the things that make you angry and sad. This lack of empathy is the main reason most of their relationships, if not all, will eventually collapse whether they are romantic or not.

It suffices to say that a relationship with this type of man will eventually end up in emotional abuse. You should get out of this relationship or marriage as soon as possible because those people have a personality disorder and need professional help, something you will not be able to provide for them.

The Romantic Man

We saved a great type of man for last. This is the romantic man. When the romance starts we are all very excited and men may go to great lengths to shower us with romance. However, as the novelty of the relationship passes, the only other time many partners see their significant other be romantic is when he proposes. How could you understand if a man is a true romantic and will offer you flowers each week?

To start with, he will remember significant dates and experiences of your relationship. He may not remember every specific detail, but he will remember all the special moments you two lived together. He will never forget an important anniversary without celebrating them and he will recall the dress you wore on your first date. He will still remember what your first vacation as a couple was and even how he proposed to you.

Another characteristic of a romantic man is that he will go out of his way to plan different things with you. Many partners complain that their husbands do not plan a little thing. Women love to be surprised and not plan every special moment no matter how small and simple. However, they are forced to because her partner will not take the initiative. So, you should actually feel lucky when your man will plan vacations, date nights, your birthday celebration, and many other things.

Another great trait of a romantic man is that he is full of pleasant surprises. Besides the fact that there are some people that hate surprises, keep in mind that this type of man has good intentions and has placed a great effort in order to surprise you because he wants to show you how special you are. Many romantic men love to surprise their partner since they love seeing the happiness and joy that fills the face of their significant other when they see the surprise.

Another trait of the romantic man is when he is acting chivalrous when he is the perfect gentleman. He will open the car door for you, he will offer you his jacket, and he will always take care of you when you are outside. Also, a romantic man is never afraid of showing his sensitive and romantic side. he may not show it to his friends or when people are with you, but he will most certainly do so when he is alone with you.

Respect is very important to a romantic man and he will show you respect every time during your life together since respect is one of the most important things to have. He will also take care of you and spoil you. By spoiling we don't necessarily mean spending a lot of money on gifts, but things such as back rubs, cooking your favorite food, massaging your feet, preparing you a bubble bath, or even bringing your favorite dessert at home.

To a romantic man, your happiness is extremely important to him and everything he does is for you due to this reason. His actions will be a constant and will not weaver, unless something serious happens. This man is also husband material, one of the great kinds.

Those were the most common types of men you will encounter and will help you determine which man is appropriate for you to build a solid marriage with. Keep in mind that a solid marriage will not exist if the relationship is not based on solid foundations first, so the type of person you are going to spend the rest of your life with is extremely important.

Chapter 3: The Different Types of Women

Just like there are different types of men, there are also different types of women. Women have been described as complicated creatures by many people, especially men, but admittedly they can have very complicated personalities or maybe men just don't know how to deal with them. Also, in many of these types, men themselves have admitted they would never choose as wife material. The truth is that men are not as keen on typing women as is the case with them.

Also, many men have admitted that they had to go through certain types of girls in order to be able to find the one and appreciate her. Admittedly, when a relationship is serious, appearance will matter less and communication will take prevalence over beauty. Let us see the different types of girls, according to experts and experience, in order to find which one is best for you to build a future together that requires a solid marriage.

The Party Girl

When you met this girl, you most certainly thought that she was the girl of your dreams. When you started dating her, you just felt so licky she accepted to be with you. She is beautiful and fabulous. However, as you keep dating her this beauty is not that appealing to you because you have noticed some traits that bother you a bit. Or maybe you love those traits and that makes you love her even more. Let us see the main characteristics of a party girl.

A party girl will always be the life of every party she is present. She will get a lot of invites to parties and when you go with her, she will already know everyone there. Why? because she is extremely familiar with the party scene. Chances are that she will introduce you to her friends, but they will ignore you since she will have their undivided attention. She revels in being the soul of the party and loves the attention as well as the thrill of the party mood.

The logical thing will be for you to want some alone time with your partner, but we don't think you will get much of it. Your girl will have to go to a party on Saturday and at a club on Friday and she needs you to go with her. She needs you to be her date, but if you are not in the mood to go this will not stop her. Partying to her is what it is most important now and a relationship will not be her first priority. She just isn't ready to give her undivided attention to being with someone since partying has won her over.

You may even be the one that nurses her back to sobriety after a hard night of partying. You may prepare an amazing breakfast for two in bed and she will just reject it asking for lots of black coffee because last night was just crazy! Then, she may start what most party girls are known for, except partying, talking about her as if you are just a prop in her life. She will make everything about her and always ask you question that has to do with her clothes and whether they look good on her or not. She will ask you if she should wear the bareback dress she likes, with black stockings or not.

Do not mistake this as her showing an interest in your opinion, she could have asked her fabulous girlfriends if you weren't there in front of her and her ticket to knowing if she is a candy in the eyes of all the other guys that will be there. She loves getting the admiration of all the guys and she will surely need to know if a dress makes her unattractive. to test this theory make a suggestion of both of you going to this party, her waring a simple everyday dress and you wearing in sweats and sneakers. A true party girl will surely think you are mad for even thinking such a thing.

Since your girl parties and is encountering hangovers every weekend chances are she will be tipsy all the time while she is at the party. She may be very fun when she is tipsy but you should think of the long term consequences of her health and make her see them. Eventually, she will get over this party obsession, but her health may already be ruined. Would you like to be with someone who is jeopardizing their health over a few parties?

One common occurrence every party girl has encountered is being taken to the police station. It will take only a call from the police that will finally and certainly show you that you got yourself a party girl. She may have been arrested on her way home because she was driving while she was drunk or she passed out in public from being too drunk. You will not be able to deny her partying habits, especially when she is partying without you.

If you are able to get past all the partying and still want to build a solid relationship with this girl that will lead to marriage, you will have to wait for this phase to end and realize that the face she is showing is a fake persona. The glittery face she is showing is essentially a shallow and fake facade that masks her insecurities, according to experts. She still doesn't know who she is or how to lead a responsible life with all the adult responsibilities. She is a flawed human like the rest of us. she is only expressing it in her own way because that is how she feels.

She is not ready at the moment for a committed, adult relationship and if you try to get her out of this phase without her really wanting it to end, you may find yourself in the future dealing with the same situation. She is not wife material, at least not yet, and the better choice for yourself is to end it unless you are not interested in a long term relationship or you like to party as much as she does.

The Daddy's Girl

The next type of woman we are going to briefly analyze is the daddy's girl. These women will show an extreme sensitivity to their dad that is beyond their age. They will ask for their father's help all the time for every insignificant situation. Essentially her partner will never measure up to her dad and when or if the relationship is over, the man will most likely feel worse than the woman, since she will have her father to assure her of her role as a princess. The following are some characteristics that show you are married or dating a daddy's girl.

This type of woman will simply not understand that the whole universe does not revolve around her. She has her father as a number one fan and for this reason, she thinks that the whole world will treat them like a princess, just like their father did. and is still doing. However, this does not apply all the various times you will meet a daddy's girl. some girls have been taught responsibilities and they are not very spoiled or they simply let only their father spoil them.

Another sign that she is a daddy's girl is that she calls her father "daddy" although her age does not call for it. Sure the term "daddy" is an endearment, but a woman will not call her father "daddy" all the time. You will also notice that she refers to her dad as a super dad. She will think that all fathers and men should be like him. She will start her sentence with "daddy says" instead of" my dad".

In the eyes of a daddy's girl, you will never be as smart as her dad. If she needs help with something, she will call her dad first, even though you may be the most successful specialist in the world about this matter. Thus, she will care more about what her father thinks than you. If you see her doing a mistake or something wrong, she will definitely be more worried about what her father will think than she is about what you will think of her.

Also, you will find some difficulties when trying to please a true daddy's girl. She has been given everything she ever wanted by her father and this is the reason why most daddy's girls are spoiled. Her needs must be immediately met whether they include your time or money. If she is not given those things, she will throw a huge tantrum and she will never appreciate anything else you do for her.

Essentially, she will act like a child. She will make a huge deal out o it and will even stop talking to you until you do what she asked of you. If you give it to her, she will hold her breath and act like a happy two-year-old. However, if you do not buy her a new car, chances are that she will ask her dad to buy it for her.

This type of woman will think that everything she does will be simply adorable. If you don't like baby voices or cute little nicknames then you are in for a treat because she will not spot doing them since she thinks they are adorable. Her father always thought she was adorable and you should think so too. His girl could never do wrong in his eyes and everything she did was adorable. Why shouldn't you think so too? She is used to being the center of attention and even if she isn't the center of your attention she will do whatever it takes to be.

If you are able to get past the daddy thing then she will make a good wife. She knows how to take care of someone, but you will need to compete pretty hard with her dad and with un-spoiling her. She will expect you to treat her like her dad did and her father will have the final say in everything. Just like the case of mama's boy.

The Independent Woman

The next type of woman we are going to analyze briefly is the independent woman. These women will be the most frank and will not fear anything to get their way. They can be easily compared to alpha males. She will need one thing to make things work and this is her independence. There are certain characteristics that will show you your woman is an independent one if you haven't figured out yet and if you do not have anyone yet, those traits will help you realize if she is the one you want to spend the rest of your life with.

First of all, you will have a hard time to win this woman over. Even for one date. This will happen because there are numerous men who will try to make a move on her, but she is very selective with whom she will go out with. She will want someone able to see that she is not just a woman among many, but an equal to the man she will choose to go out with. She needs someone to challenge her mind and reassure her that their relationship will not end as soon as they get physical.

An independent woman will motivate her partner to be the best version of himself. Whether this has to do with her partner's other relationships, career, or as a person, she will push him to be the best he could ever hope for. However, she needs her partner to understand that when there are a lot of things going on in her life, she may not have the time to see her partner as much as he would want to. When she has set goals, she wants to achieve them and for this reason, she expects her partner to be prepared to make some sacrifices.

Her friends hold her in high regard because she is strong and able to offer her support to everyone who faces emotional problems without being overwhelmed by it. She is also very passionate about the things she likes She is extremely dedicated and will never leave something unfinished. She will keep going until she finishes her task and has no intention of quitting. Also, try not to be offended when you see that she likes to do certain things alone. Independent women enjoy doing things on their own, but this will not mean that your partner does not enjoy spending time with you.

Another characteristic of this type of woman is that she is completely honest even when the truth hurts. She thinks that lying and beating around the bush is a waste of time. She will tell you everything that she feels as well as the various things she thinks about you without taking into consideration your feelings in any way. Keep in mind that she is simply honest and is not trying to hurt you. Honesty is the perfect option, even when it includes things we do not want to hear.

This type of woman is an inspiration for all other women. They look up to her and try to mimic her. Women see in her the best versions of what they can be and will actively listen to everything she has to say. She will motivate other women to be independent and achieve their goals the same way she will motivate her partner to be the best version of himself. However, keep in mind that an independent woman will not need a man to be happy. She can do just fine on her own, but she wants the man she has chosen to be beside her. She has chosen you because she saw something in you that will make both of you happy. She will not forget you under no circumstances because she loves you.

She knows what she is worth and hat she deserves and for this reason, she is not a drama queen. She is not expecting validation form the comments of other people or from the amount of money she has. She will let her actions and accomplishments speak for themselves. she loves to learn more things every day and she is always updated on the events that happen around the world. She will get attention when she knows she deserves it and this is why she doesn't care about drama. In her opinion, if you are not able to talk about something calmly and figure out a solution, there is no point in talking at all.

If her partner does something that upsets her, she will first calm down and then she will come to you to talk about it nicely. However, if her partner cheated on her, she will not talk about it, she will simply leave. No matter how much she loves you, she wants to be happy and she has decided that this cannot happen with you. as shown by your actions.

This type of woman will not apologize for who she is because she loves herself. She will be the perfect wife because you can depend on her just like she will depend on you, when the situation calls for it. She will be available to talk your problems through and find a solution that will benefit both of you. She will rarely throw any tantrums because she knows that fighting will get the relationship nowhere.

The Drama Queen

The last type of woman we are going to briefly analyze is the drama queen. When you first meet a woman that fits into this category, she will be sweet and show little signs of her demanding side. However, as time passed on, you saw more and more of this side and now the relationship may feel a full-time job since you will have to meet her every demand. Keep in mind that not every woman who will express little signs of drama will fall to this type. Let us see some characteristics of a drama queen.

She will constantly seek your attention by demanding of you to look at her. This can be during a shopping excursion when she wants your opinion on the twenty dresses she had tried on or even when you are out on a date by saying things that will make you ask her things about herself so she can talk more. When she doesn't have your undivided attention, she will throw tantrums and act as childish as she can. Drama queens think that the world revolves around them and when someone is not catering to their expectations and their needs, they will react by lashing out. Do not worry; she will make a scene even if you are out in public.

Being with her it will feel as if you are on an emotional roller coaster. This is not the fun rollercoaster, we assure you. Her moods will change from one moment to the next and the fun fact is that you will not be able to do anything about it. It is part of your relationship with her and you have adapted to the situation. Sometimes, you may find yourself wondering if she can actually see a situation from a logical point of view instead of immediately reacting based on her emotions. The simple answer is no because this will not get her closer to the things she needs and wants.

You may also have noticed that she blames you for everything wrong in her life. Not only the things that are wrong with the relationship. She may blame you for things that have to do with her work or with her friends. It doesn't matter because everything is your fault. You may also be reluctant to talk to her because you are afraid of how she will react or just tired of dealing with her emotional outbursts.

A drama queen will not forget any fight that you ever had. Usually, your fights last a week because she loves to make you guilty even if she was at fault. When you are fighting, she will remind you of all the mistakes you have ever made even if you had atoned for them a thousand times. This way she will make you feel guilty and ask for her forgiveness. Do not forget that this woman loves drama; she is the queen of it.

In most cases, your friend s and family will not like her because they can see the way she behaves around you and around them too. For this reason, she may even attempt to create drama between you and the people you love. She will attempt this by trying to manipulate your thoughts with the goal of turning your whole attention to her. Her ultimate goal will be to distance you from the people you love except her.

You will feel as if your relationship is based on a novel that is filled with drama. She loves to make grand entrances, she professes her love for you after a huge fight you had, you await her next explosion with anticipation. Don't worry; you are not the only one waiting. All the people that know you wait for it. If all these are true why people are marrying drama queens? Well, because life is boring without them. Many men have tried to break up with them because they realized the torture they had to go through, but they also loved working to please her and for her forgiveness. Men may like an easy life but some of them love drama too.

No matter which type of man or woman you are in to and think will make the perfect husband or wife or even which types you would like to avoid forever when a person meets the one he or she will know. The important thing in having a solid marriage is to construct first a solid relationship. Just because you are married it doesn't mean that everything will be great in a magical way if your relationship wasn't a good one.

Chapter 4: Build Your Relationship to Last

Every person is different and thus every relationship is different. Every relationship has different needs and expectations that are based on each partner's ability to compromise and actually be in a long term relationship with his significant other. Admittedly you are going to marry the one you want to spend the rest of your life with and you propose to make your marriage last forever, not to get divorced. Many experts agree on several characteristics that a long term healthy relationship has and will later lead to a solid marriage. However, keep in mind that those characteristics should not cease to exist after you have taken the vows. You still are in a relationship.

Relationships will be solid when both partners are not afraid to speak their mind. Couples should be able to express themselves without being afraid of the reaction of their partner. Imagine living your life without being able, to be honest about your thoughts and emotions to the only person you will live your every day with for the rest of your life. It sounds more like a cage than commitment.

Communication is essential to building a solid life together and this means that no topic is off-limits. Couples should communicate about everything and also feel comfortable in doing so. No topic is less important than others because everything, no matter how small it seems, may pose a problem in the future.

Partners in healthy and solid relationships recognize the importance of having their own space. Being in love with someone and deciding to spend the rest of your life with him or her doesn't mean that you should spend every moment of your lives together. Both partners need to have the opportunity to go after the goals they have set in life and pursue their hobbies as well as interests. Besides, when each of you pursues your interests and maintain the friendships you had prior to your union, you will keep your relationship fresh and help you grow as individuals.

Believe it or not people in healthy and solid relationships fight. They argue fairly and productively which means no insults or trying to put down your partner in order to make yourself feel good. or convince them that you are right. You are two different people that despite the fact that you are in love, have lead different lifestyles up until your union and have different beliefs or ways to deal with things. This will lead to arguments and in fact, if there are no arguments in a relationship chances are one or two partners are holding back.

By holding back, you may avoid fighting at the moment, but your pent up emotions will blow and an even greater fight will ensue with many more consequences than little arguments here and there. Obviously, for an argument to be as healthy as the relationship, the partner that is wrong should apologize and not try to make any wrong behaviors seem right.

Being in touch with reality is a very important part of building a healthy relationship. What do we mean by that? Don't start and base your relationship and marriage with the thought that things will change in the future. You know that neither you nor your partner is perfect and you accept them and love them for who they are in the present time.

You or your partner will not suddenly change by winning the lottery, moving to a new house, or having a baby. Basing your relationship to the premise that your partner will change in time and become the person of your dreams is wrong and can have many negative consequences. You love your partner because of who he or she is, not because of who they will become according to your thoughts.

Another thing couples need to understand in order to build and maintain a solid relationship and marriage is that decisions will be made by the two of you not one of you. You don't make decisions on your own and neither does your partner. Your decisions are based on mutual discussion and acceptance from how many children you will have to which movie you will see. You need to listen to the desires and needs each one of you has and try to include them both on your joint decision. If this is not possible, you compromise. For example, you may watch Star Wars on a Saturday night, but n Sunday night she will see Notebook.

A healthy relationship includes having fun with your partner and finding joy to the little moments. This doesn't mean that your partner will not get on your nerves or that you will not irritate your partner, but generally, your joint life will be most happy in the simple moments such as laughing at the same jokes, cooking dinner together or completing each other's sentences. A healthy relationship also has balance. For example, you may need to work extra hours and be the chauffeur of your children while your wife also works and deals with the house chores. This is how life is and what should matter to your relationship more is that it all seems fair to both of you. No one should take more than they can handle while the other does nothing unless the circumstances call for it.

Each partner should treat the other with empathy, care, appreciation, and consideration for a healthy relationship to take place. If by any chance, you find yourself treating other people you know with respect but not your partner, you should take a step back and rethink your relationship through. Has your partner done something to bring this behavior or is this entirely your fault? Kindness and respect are of utmost importance in a healthy and solid relationship and marriage and those traits should exist in both partners for balance to be kept.

Trust is another trait that is extremely important according to experts as well as effective communication that is indulged by both partners. A relationship should have no secrets or reservations because you have a joint life and any secrets that are kept between you may lead in the future to potential problems. Trust is the one that will allow us to open up to a partner and share many details of our lives and problems that we need help with. According to Marissa Gomez Schursky, who is a marriage and family therapist, "Trust is what allows us to be vulnerable, and vulnerability is key in blossoming relationships. As trust grows in a relationship, partners feel safe with each other, and that safety results in more transparency between individuals."

In a relationship, one partner will annoy the other as well as say things they don't necessarily mean. These things are completely normal in a healthy relationship since we're dealing with two individual people that will eventually behave inconsiderably. The most important thing that people who are in a long-term relationship and want to build a solid marriage need to understand is how to effectively deal with all these situations. You need to know how to let things go and even if your partner forgot to pick up coffee for the third time this month, tell them that you are disappointed but then let it go. There is no need to fight over something as simple as this.

The physical part of a healthy relationship is very important, but intimacy may be even more important than sex. Intimacy is all about familiarity, bonding, and friendship. When you are in a healthy relationship you must feel connected to your partner even when you are out of bed. A healthy relationship must make you feel secure and happy. It must provide you with a place t return to at the end of the day and relax. This does not mean that you will not fight with your partner or that things will not be hard sometimes, but despite all, your partner will be your rock and you will prefer to see your partner than anyone else.

Also, in a healthy relationship that is based on effective communication, you will mostly want to speak to your partner and not to other people. You would prefer to share your concerns and problems with your partner and not your coworkers. However, this will not mean that you will not have friends, but your friends should not be your escape route so as to not speak with the one you are with about the various things that trouble you or make you happy.

Another important thing to remember is that saying the magic words "Thank you", "I love you", and "I am sorry", is also an essential part of a healthy relationship, no matter how long you are with your partner. Even if you are with him or her, a couple of years or 50 years, those words will always shed a new light on your relationship. By showing as well as assuring our partner with words about our feelings we will make ourselves and the other person happy to be with you and to have chosen to share their lives with you.

Transparency is also another essential characteristic when it comes to healthy relationships. Being open to your partner about your past as well as your needs of the future will help you both grow. For example, by sharing your past you, as well as your partner, will realize how much you have matured and not to mention that this will help him or her realize more of the things that made you the person your partner loves today.

Besides, holding things in, it will not do your relationship any good since you will pressure yourself and it will essentially mean that you are not comfortable talking with your partner since transparency means that you are able to talk with your partner about topics that make you both uncomfortable According to Marissa Gomez Schursky "Ask yourself if you feel open to being honest with your partner rather than feeling like you need to hold things in". If you are able to give an affirmative response to this, then your relationship has one more important characteristic of a healthy relationship.

For a long term relationship and marriage to last forever, compromise is essential. With compromise partners show that they are open to the perspective of the other and thus show their respect for the needs of each individual that is a part of this relationship. The needs of both of you will not always be the same, so in order to reach a solution that you both agree to, you need to compromise. This is also a sign of respect that will be an integral part of your long term happiness. In the words of specialist Marissa Gomez Schursky "Compromising encourages people to hear one another out rather than critiquing. It's a positive sign if a couple finds they can both slow down and share their opinions, even when they're opposing."

As a couple, you will argue. A healthy argument, however, should end with the identification of different resolutions and reach a complete end once you find the solution that will satisfy both partners. However, you should not leave problems unsolved because they will appear later, maybe with more force that will create an even more intense argument than before. Keep in mind that a healthy relationship includes the solution of problems and not ignoring them until they grow and ultimately become unsolvable.

It would also be good for your relationship to make time and talk about it as if you were discussing a third person. This way you will give both the opportunity to confess any troubles you are facing based on the relationship, worries, or unresolved issues you think that exists. During this time, be careful not to pas any judgments or create arguments because this is the time where you let your relationship grow and become better, healthier. Another thing that can make your relationship turn into a healthy one and let it grow is to remind yourself and your partner the time when you fell in love. for example, you can remember old stories of the two of you and look at old pictures. Realize how much you have grown as well as your relationship through those memories and keep in mind that we all are a result of r experiences. During the years you are together you have managed to grow into the relationship and this is another characteristic of a healthy relationship. It helps you grow as a person and as a couple.

A healthy relationship will require from each partner to set goals as well as to keep track of them. A relationship is like everything else you love doing and value. It needs a plan, work, and if something doesn't go to plan, review. Also, it would be good for you and your partner to share small adventures since your life may turn into a boring routine. You could start small by going together for coffee or shopping or even go for a walk in nature and the beach. This way you will keep your relationship healthy by not letting your stress from everyday responsibilities spoil your union.

Also, a healthy relationship involves the two partners to encourage each other to try new things. For example, one partner may want to do something but was hesitant to start at first. A healthy relationship is also based on the premise that each partner helps the other be a better person and support him or her in making the dreams of the partner a reality. You could do this y joining your partner into a new hobby he or she wants to start and who knows? You might actually love it yourself. Not to mention the benefit that you will spend time together doing things you have never done before.

Another trait of a healthy relationship is the fact that sometimes people change. What we can control when this happens is the way we change. For example, change is good when you or your partner learn from your past mistakes and try to not repeat them again as well as change the certain characteristics that led you to make this mistake. You could think of the different reasons why you and your partner made this mistake and stop repeating it. We are human and we all make mistakes. However, in a healthy relationship, we learn from them and help the relationship grow past it. If we keep repeating the same mistakes over and over again, this behavior will have detrimental effects on your relationship.

In a healthy relationship, partners are also friends. This is why the person you will share the rest of your life with becomes the one who will support you, respect you, love you, and share your troubles as well as your happiness. By being friends too, you will be able to very comfortable with each other and share your inner and deepest thoughts. Your partner will be the person who is affected the most by changes in your life since he or she lives with you and spends years being by your side. The same goes for the different events that happen in your partner's life affect you and you would like to know the different problems they face so as to deal with them together.

Also, in a healthy relationship, both partners should know when it is the right time to say "no" even if this is a hard thing to do. Every relationship has its limitations and you should both be able to recognize the situation that will place your relationship in danger and avoid them altogether. Partners need to be realistic and avoid situations that will endanger the relationship and ultimately break it up. For example, indulging in an expensive lifestyle that is not appropriate for the economic situation of the couple while you want to settle down and buy a house will surely affect the relationship if both partners are not able to control themselves and set their priorities straight. Both partners should have realistic plans and expectations when they want to build a life together.

Building a healthy relationship can be a lot of work, but you will have to do what it takes to succeed because nothing good in life was earned by slanginess. You want to share the rest of your life with this person and in order to achieve this; you will need solid foundations based on which this will happen. You work hard to make money and live a comfortable life and you build a strong house to live safely. Why should relationships be different? The work that is placed in solidifying your life with another person will be rewarding for both of you since your life will include fewer problems and the effective communication that is required to solve any troubling situation that comes your way.

Chapter 5: Common Troubles in Marriages

Many marriages end in divorce nowadays for various reasons. The time we live in now has changed dramatically the way people deal with relationships as well as tying the knot and a big part for the dissolution of a union is the pace of our lives as well as personal choices. Unfortunately, divorce is the norm now and the number of people who decide to salvage their marriage lessens with every year that passes. According to studies conducted by sociologists, divorce rates increase by year and the number of couples that follow the divorce route has doubled over the past 40 years.

But why is this happening? An average time span that a marriage lasts nowadays is from 7 to 10 years and the most common reasons that couples get a divorce remain the same in every country and include infidelity, egoism, financial problems, and lack of communication between the two partners. Also, those studies have shown that women will decide on divorce more often than men do. According to psychologists, this happens because women are more emotional and analytical than men and thus they take matters more seriously. Women are free to choose their fate since their rights are safer now and will leave their husbands easier than they could in the past.

We will present you with some of those problems so as to spot them and fix them before they lead you on the path of divorce. While it is true that divorce sometimes is inevitability, on the occasions that the relationship can be saved, it is worth to work hard and save the life you share with your partner.

One common mistake married couples do is overstepping the boundaries of their relationship by trying to change their partner. They may be focused on the partner's beliefs or fashion sense. No matter the change they want to make on their partner, this is a clear invasion of their personality and their personal space. This situation will lead to the spouse that is subjected to this behavior to eel angry, disrespected, or even hurt.

The fact that a partner would want to change the other is a violation of mutual respect, especially when it is done intentionally with a goal in mind. The partner that is subjected to the desire of the other spouse to change him or her, may retaliate and even turn away from the relationship. As a result, it will be hard for both partners to keep respecting, communication, be open, and love each other. The best way to avoid this before it brings about very serious consequences is to communicate your feelings to the partner that trying to change you and draw a clear line that cannot be crossed. No one should try to change who you are and most importantly explain to them that by trying to change you they show that they do not love you since love means accepting our partner for whom he or she is.

Another serious problem couples may face during their marriage is lack of communication. You need to understand that talking and communicating are two totally different things. Talking includes the exchange of information without the necessary response of the partner and as such, it leaves the conversation open to criticism and complaining.

Communicating includes the nonverbal and verbal exchange of information that essentially needs a response. You also need more than one person to communicate and is mainly focused on the bond of two people having a conversation that does not include judgment.

Communication is essential for the couple to speak effectively and understand the needs of each partner. Couples should build a solid foundation through which they will be able to communicate effectively otherwise problems will arise that cannot be faced when two people who share a life together are not able to understand each other.

Moving on, when people are married and as responsibilities grow, it is easy to face the common problem of turning their attention away from each other and their relationship to other things such as hobbies, career, social activities, children, or friends. Many people believe that since they are married, they no longer need to work on the relationship and are justified to ignore their partner in order to do other things. Loss of attention is a serious reason many marriages fail and in such cases, it is not uncommon for one partner to feel as if he or she is living with a roommate and not a lover.

The truth is that relationships, including married couples, need continuous care and attention. Couples need to find a balance between giving attention to your partner's needs and personal interest. Spouses should have their own interests that are separated from the relationship but not at the expense of their partner that will feel neglected. Couples need to spend quality time together and for as long as this happens the problems that occur with any lack of attention will not trouble you and your relationship.

The reaction of many people when they see that their partner is not paying attention to them is to overreact by telling their partner that they should not have personal interest without them. It suffices to say that this reaction will create more problems in the relationship than you will be able to deal with. Talk with your partner and try to understand that your significant other is now pursuing his goals in life now that he has finally found the one for him or her and has settled.

Another common problem that married couples face is emotional infidelity. There are many cases of people who get emotionally disconnected from one another after they are married. When this problem occurs, the needs of one spouse, if not the needs of both, will not be satisfied and he or she may start searching for their fulfillment somewhere else. This is how emotional infidelity happens because it found an opportunity to enter the marriage.

There have been many reports from married couples that decided to attend therapy sessions to salvage their marriage that emotional infidelity is way worse than the physical one. The reason why this is the case is that emotional infidelity is more than sex as it happens in physical infidelity. With emotional infidelity, you are able to connect with someone else intimately. In order for you to avoid this situation, you need to be clear on what each of you considers as cheating.

One or both partners may consider cheating to be only on a physical level, but by making it clear that emotional infidelity is off-limits too it will lessen the chances of happening. Keep in mind that attending to the emotional needs of your partner it is extremely important in a solid marriage because they will not get interested in having their needs met with another person.

Money can also be a sore spot for many married couples that will lead to arguments and end in divorce. When two partners bond, often their bank accounts bond too. Even if you keep your finances separate, economic problems may still pose a problem to your relationship since there will be things you will need to buy together or communicate on how to spend your money as a married couple.

To avoid those problems you need to discuss how you will handle money as a couple with your partner sine both of you have different spending habits and way of handling your money. This matter can be a sore spot and lead to tense conversations, so it is not uncommon for the discussion to become more about personal habits and less about money.

For example, if one partner is stressed about money, they may pic a fight with their spouse about unrelated things without even realizing it. For this reason, try each month to make a budget and calculate your revenues and expenses. Make a financial plan and try to stick to it as faithfully as possible. This way you will be more in control of the money issue and will not let turn into a huge problem that will affect your relationship.

We live in a world where technology has become an essential part of our lives and many people tend to forget the importance of human communication and contact. Technology can pose a big problem for married couples and relationships in general since there are more reports from couples that one partner is obsessed with technology and he or she lets it get in the way of their marriage. How is this possible, you may ask. Let us see an example.

You are having dinner with your wife or husband, but he or she is so focused on her or his smartphone that she is browsing through the internet or texting friends instead of engaging in a productive conversation with you. Maybe they are even playing games through your shared time together instead of taking an interest in your day and giving you the attention that is required thought the times you spend together.

On these occasions, communication and intimacy which are required for a healthy and solid marriage are placed in danger and can lead to many arguments and create problems between the couple. We come across people that are glued to their smartphones every day, so if this is happening to your marriage too, it is time to talk to your partner about it and if he or she is addicted, you should both discuss the option of getting your partner some professional help.

Selfishness is another reason that many marriages end in divorce. Selfishness occurs in a marriage when one spouse places his or her needs above the ones of his or her partner constantly. If this is a common occurrence, it will not be long until the affected partner will feel unloved and unworthy, thus turning the marriage into a tortured one instead of being a healthy and solid marriage. When two people decide to get married they do so out of love and respect for each other and this includes the promise of not being selfish towards the one we love.

Selfishness comes in many forms and shapes such as manipulation, controlling behaviors possessiveness and jealousy. When it is not that strong it will include a lack of respect and consideration that have to do with the emotions and needs of your partner. Effective communication can help you in such cases as well as learning how to act with empathy towards your partner sine being in a relationship means that the needs of both partners need to be met.

Problems in a married couple can occur when there is no trust between them. Trust is one of the fundamental bases for love and without it no healthy marriage or a relationship, in general, will exist. When one partner breaks his or her promises, lies, and cheats he or she will damage the relationship, sometimes beyond repair. When trust is gone, restoring it in a marriage is not an easy thing to do and it needs the commitment of both parties for any hope to exist to salvage this union.

If the issues that contribute to the lack of trust to occur are not dealt with effectively, then the affected partner will keep feeling suspicious, angry, and hurt, thus leading probably to the end of the union because as time passes those emotions will grow and be more intense, thus eliminating any chances of saving the relationship.

117

Troubles when dealing with anger effectively can also create problems in a marriage. It is normal for couples to fight and get angry at each other. However, it is not common to not be able to control this anger appropriately when these situations arise. Some people are not able to control their anger and react explosively with fits of rage that will not help the relationship at all and if those occurrences are frequent will lead to a divorce since the affected partner will not be able to deal with such behaviors.

For this reason, it is extremely important for couples to not discuss important matters when they are angry and only when they have calmed down. Keep in mind that when having such delicate discussions, you should take into consideration the feelings of your partner as well as your own. Each partner should be able to express their opinions openly and listen to their views that are related to the problem at hand. Also, you should avoid defensive behaviors.

Usually, people who have decided that they want to get married and share their lives together have discussed already how they want their future to be before they get married. However, there have been many cases where one or both partners have changed their minds and decided to set different goals and plans as time passed and this is another common problem among couples. Let us see an example. You and your partner got married and had decided before that you want to buy a house, have kids, and start a family.

However, after your honeymoon, one of you decides that they want to travel the world, study or doesn't want to have kids anymore then you would have some major issues to deal with. There is no reason to argue intensely about this or worry that your relationship will change drastically since your partner changed his or her mind. Remember that communication is the key to such situations and it would be better to figure out a new plan with the new data you have. Life is not set in stone and there is a solution for almost every problem.

When we love someone we decide to stay committed to that person. Essentially marriage is the decision to stay with our partner through the happy and difficult moments and the strength of the emotions of a partner in love is shown through the difficult times in life. However, studies have shown that even though people still hold the belief that family lasts forever, people get married, have children, and when they reach a certain age, they get divorced. This is happening because life expectancy has grown since the last century and people do not know where they will be in 20 years for now.

For example, a woman is 25-28 old when she is married and the man is 28-32. People will think that it will be difficult for those partners to stay married for 40-45 years since people can change as well as situations. According to experts, people will set different goals in life and people are not able to predict the various responsibilities they will face when they get married. This is the reason why, when they reach a certain age, they get divorced.

In today's world, there are many temptations that can drive a couple apart since technology has made it easier to meet new people. Despite the many temptations, it would be wise to think of the reasons why you fell in love with your partner in the first place and try to renew your relationship by paying more attention to your partner and having new experiences together than ruining the relationship you and your partner tried so hard to build.

There many ways to keep the relationship strong and show your partner that you care about them as well as how much you value them. When the years pass many people tend to forget to take care of their appearance when in the presence of their partner. When kids arrive along with the added responsibilities, both partners may walk around in sweatpants and even without brushing their teeth because they had a very difficult night.

However, this is not going to make your partner think of you as attractive as he or she used to. It may sound shallow, but this is the truth. Attractiveness is part, no matter how small, of the reason you are with this person and should not change even after ten years of you two being together. We are not saying that you should look beautiful and fresh 24/7, but simple things like taking care of your hair, wearing more carefully chosen clothes when you two are together will make a great improvement in the way your partner sees you.

Also, you could watch what you are saying when you are in the presence of your partner. For example, you will not say to her that you think the new neighbor is attractive. Also, you shouldn't start sentences with the words "You never..." You always..." because they just look bad unless you want to say "You are always beautiful," You never look tired t me". Expressing the things that bother you, should more carefully thought since the way you express things, even negative ones, will have a detrimental effect on the course of the discussion.

Remember to be kind to your partner and keep the passion as well as the intimacy, inside and outside of your bedroom. Sometimes we tend to take advantage of the person we love, mostly without intending to, because we know he or she loves us and will let us get away with it. For example, you were angry at something that happened to your work and you return home and take out to your partner.

If this is happening constantly, take care because this behavior has to change. Even if your partner says nothing, you will end up a selfish person that takes continues advantage of your partner. Instead, think that you are returning home to your loving partner that will help you relax and get over the stress you had to go through at work.

Keep in mind that all relationships go through hard times and for this reason couples should stick together. The difficult times are the ones that will determine if the relationship will hold and result in a solid marriage since those are considered the tests of how strong is the bond that the couple has created.

Chapter 6: Things You Should Do Before Marriage

You have reached a place where you know who is the one you want to spend the rest of your life with. You popped the question and now you are preparing for the big day. However, there are a few things you should consider doing before starting officially your lives together. Let us take a better look at what are those things.

Before getting married, you should clarify which are the career goals of you and your partner. You need to talk about the different things you wish to accomplish in your life and how those things will affect your relationship. Supporting the dreams of your partner and your partner supporting your goals is an essential part of having a sild marriage. Besides, what a better motivator to succeed than the support of the one you love?

The next thing you should talk about is money and the spending habits each of you has. This discussion includes any debt you or your partner may have as well as your saving plans. However, if you have different spending habits it doesn't mean that your marriage is going to fail as long as your responsibilities are taken care of and there is money left for you to be comfortable.

Another discussion you need to have before tying the knot is whether you want children or no as well as when you should have them. Starting a family should be a common decision and a general plan should be discussed before marriage. By getting married it doesn't necessarily mean that your partner wants to have children, so before making more wedding plans keep in the back of your mind that you should also pop up this question too. Also, you shouldn't have to agree on how many children you want just yet. According to Jaclyn Bronstein who is a mental health counselor in New York, "Once a couple has their first kid, they will have a better idea of how many children they really want."

You should also talk about the past each of you had and the important things that affected your life. Like it or not, your past played a big role on who you are today and the same principle applies to your partner too. It doesn't matter that there are things in your past you are ashamed of. Your partner surely has some too and it will not hinder him or her from telling you about it. This discussion should include the existence of any previous spouses or children that may come from this previous marriage.

Also, you should talk about how each other response to stressful situations. Your partner may have seen how you react to stress since they have lived with you for a while, but hearing you talk about it as well as giving away some useful tips will be an added bonus to building your solid marriage. Many marriages end up in divorce because stressful situations have not been dealt with effectiveness that comes from effective communication.

It would be good to figure out how to talk to each other. Not through emails, phones, or texts because your most important conversations as a married couple will occur through face to face contact. Any uncomfortable conversations you will have will be dealt with accordingly and with effectiveness if you have cleared beforehand how each partner faces various serious problems. You don't only have to talk about how you should speak to each other through difficult situations, you could only talk about the various habits you have when communicating that gets on each other's nerves or love.

Another thing you should do before getting married to the one you love is to live with him or her. This way you will be able to see which are the habits your partner has that will annoy you the most and deal with them before things get out of hand. There are many traits your partner will have that you will find out during that time and may annoy you too much for you to be able to handle. There have been many reports of couples constantly arguing about small habits that have been an integral part of their partner's lives when they lived alone. The key here is compromise. When we live with someone else, we should take into consideration the things that annoy him or her and try to fix them. Just like your partner should do about the things that will annoy you.

If you re both working, then it should be wise to have a discussion about dividing up the chores of your house. You wouldn't want your house to be constantly a mess because neither partner will be too tired to tide up the place. Even if you think that dividing the chores is not a serious matter, you will find out that there will be arguments later because you didn't take out the trash and your house smells. So, try to fair and help each other out when it comes to house chores because this could potentially be a source of argument.

Another thing you should do before getting married is to plan a big trip together. Whether you believe it or not this trip will be a source of stress for both of you since you will have to book a hotel room and plane tickets as well as organize your budget for this trip. This will be a perfect exercise that will somewhat show you how to handle your future shared responsibility. Also, when you reach your destination, you will have to make various decisions on where to go, what to do while you are there, and where you should spend your money. A trip will be a true eye opener.

When you are getting married to someone the most essential thing you will need to accept and realize is that you will share a future you will create together, you will have a common purpose.

If you want different things, you will never be able to unite so as to achieve this common purpose.

However, if you have successfully managed to plan a future together, you will have to make compromises, deal effectively with the various problems that will arise through effective communication and share your thoughts with your partner. Be honest and true to your significant other and do not take advantage of his or her love for you. A solid marriage will make you the happiest person in the world if it is treated with the respect it deserves.

Conclusion

Being married to someone can either turn out to be a blessing or a curse. It will be a curse if you aren't sure about the person we are with as well as that he or she wants the same things or similar things out of life as you do. It will also be a curse if you do not treat your partner with the respect he or she deserves. Do not forget that a solid marriage comes from a healthy and solid relationship, so before you head to take the next step, try to solidify your relationship first. There will come the time when you will know that your connection with your partner is so strong that it will be able to be turned into a successful marriage.

Your partner will not be afraid to challenge you since he or she will kindly make his or her views clear concerning the various things that have to do with you and your relationship. According to relationship expert and psychotherapist Rhonda Richards-Smith, "If your partner is comfortable enough with you to lovingly call you out privately when they feel you are wrong, chances are you are in the right relationship."

Also, you will allow one another some personal space due to the fact that will trust each other too much. If this happens, then your relationship will be heading for a successful marriage. You and your partner will understand the need to have individual hobbies, interests, friends and time for yourselves.

Enjoying various things outside the relationship will help each person to develop and grow and thus the relationship will grow too. In the word of Richards-Smith, "There's nothing worse than feeling smothered or obligated to track your partner's every move, If you are both able to trust one another enough to have your own time, space, and friends, you're on the right track." Your relationship will turn into a solid marriage as long as you keep this behavior going throughout your marriage too.

You will know that your relationship will be translated into a successful marriage when you both realize that the other is not perfect, however, they are perfect to you. This realization will be based on realistic expectations and on the premise that will not wish for your partner to change after you say the magic words that will have you being married to each other. Your partner should not have to change because you love them as they are.

Thinking that they will change as time passes and become your perfect spouse is a serious indicator that not only you shouldn't get married but to re-evaluate your whole relationship too. Essentially as Lori Salkin says, a matchmaker and dating coach "There will always be someone more attractive, successful, and so on," she shares. "But what's important is to realize that you are not perfect and this other person may not be either, but together, you are perfect for each other."

When your relationship is on a one-way path for marriage you will be the biggest cheerleader of your partner and the same will be true for your partner. You will both be the biggest support to your individual goals and will want to bring out the best version your partner can be just as your partner will bring out the best in you. According to family and marriage therapist Marissa Nelson, "You encourage one another's individual growth and give support to the pursuit of each other's dreams and career aspirations. If one of you succeeds, you both win, and that level of strength over time can be a telling sign that engagement is on the horizon." Having someone who supports your goals with such fervor means that you will never fail since your partner will be there to help you through the most difficult times you will encounter and will never let you give up.

When you have a solid marriage, you will enjoy many benefits and the most important one will be having a person next to you that ill have your back and support you no matter what. You will have someone who will tell you when you are being stubborn and will try to protect you from making many mistakes throughout your life. You will be able to be yourself and show your vulnerabilities to someone who will love both your strengths and faults.

According to Marissa Nelson, "Your partner sees you at your worst and best, and loves you unconditionally, flaws and all. You take good care of one another and look out for your partner's well-being with thoughtfulness, kindness, and compassion. It's one the main qualities that let people know this person is the right one for them." What more could someone want than spend their lives with someone who will make you the best version of yourself? Marriage is not as easy as some people make it seem, but the best things in life are achieved through hard work.

www.ingramcontent.com/pod-product-compliance
Lightning Source LLC
Chambersburg PA
CBHW050734030426
42336CB00012B/1558